ARCO

D0337970

HOW TO
INTERPRET
Poetry

Laurie E. Rozakis, Ph.D.

The State University of New York

DISCARD

MISSION BRANCH

MACMILLAN • USA

Contents

Acknowledgments

"Ars Poetica" from *Collected Poems 1917–1982* by Archibald MacLeish. Copyright © 1985 by The Estate of Archibald MacLeish. Reprinted by permission of Houghton Mifflin Co. All rights reserved.

"Among School Children" and "Sailing to Byzantium" reprinted with permission of Simon & Schuster from *The Poems of W.B. Yeats: A New Edition,* edited by Richard J. Finneran. Copyright 1928 by Macmillan Publishing Company, renewed 1956 by Georgie Yeats.

"Design" and "Fire and Ice" from *The Poetry of Robert Frost,* edited by Edward Connery Lathem. Copyright 1936, 1951 by Robert Frost. Copyright © 1964 by Lesley Frost Ballantine. Copyright 1923 © 1969 by Henry Holt and Co., Inc. Reprinted by permission of Henry Holt and Co., Inc.

Introduction

WHY POETRY?

Poetry is universal to all people, all places, all times. The most unlettered people have memorized poetry; the most cultured have nurtured it. Poetry knows no barriers, neither culture, age, gender, nor religion. We can even make a case that poetry captures the rhythm of the universe, the ebb and flow of the tides, the relentless beat of the seasons, the rise and fall of our breath. Why is poetry the closest thing humanity has to a universal language? First of all, poetry delights the ear, mind, and soul. It satisfies our craving for beauty and music through the power of its language.

But poetry conveys more than mere pleasure; it also communicates meaning. Good poetry offers food for the soul, a sense that we are linked through all time by the eternal verities. We value poetry for what it reveals about our inner selves and outer lives. "Poetry," wrote the Nobel Prize–winning poet T.S. Eliot, "may make us from time to time a little more aware of the deeper, unnamed feelings to which we rarely penetrate."

Poetry reveals these "deeper, unnamed feelings" common to everyone. Poetry interprets our hidden emotions and gives them voice. By calling attention to the aspects of life we might overlook in our hurry, poetry makes us understand not only their nature but also our own. As a result, poetry is not something special or set apart from our daily lives. Rather, it is an integral part of everyone, an expression of our deepest hopes, wishes, and dreams.

FEAR OF POETRY

Although poetry satisfies a deep human appetite, many people fear and distrust it. Poetry is difficult to understand, they claim, obscure and strange. Poetry is written by men and women out of touch with the realities of life, esthetes chambered in an ivory tower, these people claim. Even though such fears have little grounding in truth, they persist. In fact, from the earliest times, most poets have been people of action, deeply involved with the rhythms of common life. Elizabethan poet Ben Jonson was a bricklayer and Scottish bard Robert Burns, a farmer. American poet Walt Whitman was a carpenter and teacher; E.A. Robinson worked in the New York subways. Herman Melville made his living in a New York City customhouse; William Carlos Williams was a physician; Langston Hughes worked as a hotel busboy. Nor are female poets sheltered from the rigors of life: Phillis Wheatley was a former slave and Stevie Smith a secretary. Today, Adrienne Rich teaches in colleges around the country.

Ironically, many poets fear their readers as much as some readers fear poetry. Emily Dickinson, for example, was well aware of the risk involved in revealing her soul through her poetry. Here's how she voiced her hopes and fears:

This is my letter to the world

This is my letter to the World
That never wrote to Me—
The simple News that Nature told—
With tender Majesty

Her Message is committed
To Hands I cannot see
For love of Her—Sweet—countrymen—
Judge tenderly—of Me

Dickinson so feared the prejudice against poetry that she published only seven poems during her lifetime. More than a thousand of her poems were found in a shoebox after her death.

WHAT IS POETRY?

Many poets have tried to define their craft. "Prose," claimed Samuel Taylor Coleridge, "consists of words in their best order. Poetry consists of the *best* words in the *best* order." Edgar Allan Poe believed that poetry was "the rhythmical creation of beauty"; to Robert Frost, it was "a reaching out toward expression, an effort to find fulfillment." Frost saw a complete poem as one where "an emotion has found its thought and the thought has found the words." According to Matthew Arnold, "Poetry is simply the most beautiful, the most impressive, and the most effective mode of saying things." Percy Bysshe Shelley wrote that "Poetry is the record of the best and happiest moments of the best minds, the very image of life expressed in its eternal truth."

Twentieth-century poet Archibald MacLeish defined poetry this way:

Ars Poetica

A poem should be palpable and mute
As a globed fruit,

Dumb
As old medallions to the thumb,

Silent as the sleeve-worn stone
Of casement ledges where moss has grown—

A poem should be wordless
As the flight of birds.
*

A poem should be motionless in time
As the moon climbs,

Leaving, as the moon releases
Twig by twig the night-entangled trees,

Leaving, as the moon behind the winter leaves,
Memory by memory the mind—

A poem should be motionless in time
As the moon climbs.
*

A poem should be equal to:
Not true.

For all the history of grief
An empty doorway and a maple leaf.

For love
The leaning grasses and two lights above the sea—

A poem should not mean
But be.

As MacLeish was well aware, poetry is a way to use language to say more than the simple words themselves. It communicates a significant experience shared by many by allowing us to become a part of that experience. Many of the experiences poetry depicts are beautiful, but not all, for poetry is not restricted to the lovely. Rather, its range includes all of human experience, the ugly as well as the exquisite, the harsh as well as the soothing. Poetry is a rhythmical expression of words that contain a deeply felt emotion. Poetry embraces all aspects of life and takes on all comers.

READING POETRY

When we analyze poems, we explore the words to see how they move—and how they move us. When our initial excitement subsides, it's time to take a close look at the inner workings of the poet's art. In this book, you'll learn how to analyze a poem to understand and appreciate its craftsmanship. You'll explore such poetic devices as rhyme, rhythm, figurative language, diction, allusions, imagery, voice, and irony. Why did the poet select one word over another? Why did the poet arrange the words in just that way?

Ah, you say, I enjoy reading poetry but I don't like all this stuff about metaphors and similes, alliteration and assonance. I don't want to strip away the veils to see what's underneath. Rest easy; the magic of poetry will remain. Only your understanding will increase.

HOW TO USE THIS BOOK

This book is divided into eight chapters. We recommend that you read through each chapter in order, since each part builds on the preceding one. We start at the beginning, with a detailed discussion of reading and interpreting poetry.

Chapter 1 provides a general overview of reading and interpreting poetry. Here, you will learn how to understand a poem by following the punctuation and other clues to meaning, such as symbols and allusions. Detailed explanations take you step by step through the learning process. You'll study important poems by well-respected writers such as Nobel Laureate W.B. Yeats.

Chapter 2 explains how to follow a poem's *meter*, or beat. In this chapter, you'll learn all about the four types of verse: *accentual, syllabic, accentual-syllabic,* and *free verse*. Detailed charts, extensive examples, and clear explanations will help you probe the underpinnings of the poet's art. At the end of the chapter, you'll find a complete review of everything you explored. Study the chart to reinforce what you have learned.

Chapter 3, "Rhyme and Figurative Language," takes you on a guided tour through each different kind of rhyme and all the figures of speech. First, you will learn all about *alliteration, assonance, consonance, euphony, cacophony, eye-rhyme, half-rhyme, internal rhyme, masculine and feminine rhyme,* and *true* or *perfect rhyme*. Each aspect of rhyme is explained completely as well as illustrated with passages from important poems. This is followed by a section on figurative language. Here, you will learn about each figure of speech. The figures of speech are arranged alphabetically for ease of use. Later, you can use these sections as handy reference guides when you read poetry on your own.

Chapter 4 takes you through types of poems and important poetic movements. Read this section through from beginning to end to see how each poetic theory developed from the preceding one. Once again, all explanations are backed up with specific examples from famous poems.

Chapter 5, "How Poets Create a Vision," explores the three basic parts of any poem: its vision, the speaker who expresses that vision, and the language the poet uses to express voice and vision. In this chapter, you will learn how poets create a vision in their work—and how you can discover and appreciate that vision. Here, you'll test your knowledge by analyzing a series of poems. Probing questions guide you to synthesize all you have learned. Each exercise is followed by complete answers so you can check your work. After you complete an exercise, go back and review anything you did not understand.

Chapter 6 explores rhymed and unrhymed verse, starting with accentual verse, blank verse, and free verse, and moving to specific kinds of rhymed verse. You'll find explanations and examples of narrative poems, lyrics, odes, and sonnets. Once again, detailed line-by-line explanations and guided questions and answers make it easy for you to understand and appreciate different types of poetry.

Chapter 7 is a series of sample essays for analysis. Each poem is followed by a question and sample essay. There's even an explanation of why each essay answers the question. This will help you model your own responses on sample papers and to understand why your own essays do or do not answer the questions.

Chapter 8 provides a detailed recommended reading list, including poetry from ancient times to today. The list contains more than one hundred recognized poets from all countries. Included are poets from America, England, Europe, Africa, Israel, South America, Latin America, India, Mexico, Russia, and the Caribbean. Use this list to discover more of the joys of poetry.

Enjoy!

Chapter 1

How to Read and Interpret Poetry

While there are different methods of approaching poetry, there are some general guidelines that have proven helpful for many readers. Try these steps:

1. Read the poem through once and see how much of the author's meaning you can immediately grasp.
2. Then go back through the poem a second time, line by line. Define all the images and symbols, if necessary referring to outside reference works or to other poems by the same author.
3. If you are still having difficulty understanding the poem, consider "translating" each line into prose. Or substitute simpler words for more difficult ones.
4. When you understand all the basic words and ideas in the poem, reread the poem a few more times and pull it all back together.

FOLLOW THE PUNCTUATION

Poetry will make a great deal more sense if you read it in an everyday speaking tone, letting the accents fall where they seem natural. Pay attention to the punctuation the author uses, ending a line only when the punctuation indicates that it is correct to do so. The punctuation marks in poetry tell us how the author wishes the work to be read. For example, a period or an exclamation mark can be thought of as a complete stop, while a comma, in contrast, would be a pause or a half-stop. As a result, there is no need to stop at the end of a line of poetry unless

1

there is some punctuation mark to indicate that we must. Here's a sample of what we mean:

> Farewell, too little, and too lately known,
> Whom I began to think and call my own;
> For sure our souls were near allied, and thine
> Cast in the same poetic mold with mine.

These first four lines of John Dryden's poem "To the Memory of Mr. Oldham" show several uses of the pause. When a line of verse has a pause as its end, as in "known," "own," and "mine," the line is called *end-stopped*. Pauses within a line, as after the words "little" and "allied," are called *caesuras*. The term means "little pause." When there is no pause at the end of a line, as in line 3 of this example, one line flows into the next. The line is called a *run-on line* or an *enjambment*. These effects are especially common in modern verse.

When you read poetry, follow the poet's directions. Do not insert punctuation where none is indicated, and do not force a word to be stressed that would not normally be so. Some poets, such as Gerard Manley Hopkins, frequently indicate to readers that a certain word should be stressed by the addition of a stress mark. Readers, of course, should follow such directions. Some lines may be read in more than one way, depending, for example, on the reader's background. A poem read by a Southerner might sound very different from one read by a New Englander, for instance. Use your common sense and pronounce each line as you would normally speak, and the poem will make a great deal more sense.

LOOK FOR SYMBOLS, ALLUSIONS, AND OTHER CLUES TO MEANING

Since poetry is so highly condensed, most poets construct meaning by aligning words in new and interesting ways, drawing on conventional symbols and *allusions* (references), and even creating private symbols of their own. You should not have too much difficulty understanding conventional allusions and symbols; if you do, nearly all can be easily looked up in a dictionary, encyclopedia, or other reference text. Private symbols can be more difficult to understand. In these instances, see how the images relate to the rest of the poem. Draw together all the different parts of the poem as you would a jigsaw puzzle to find the missing piece.

Let's apply the suggestions outlined above to the reading and interpretation of the poems that follow.

Sailing to Byzantium

1

That is no country for old men. The young
In one another's arms, birds in the trees
—Those dying generations—at their song,
The salmon-falls, the mackerel-crowded seas,
Fish, flesh, or fowl, commend all summer long
Whatever is begotten, born, and dies.
Caught in that sensual music all neglect
Monuments of unageing intellect.

2

An aged man is but a paltry thing,
A tattered coat upon a stick, unless
Soul clap its hands and sing, and louder sing
For every tatter in its mortal dress,
Nor is there singing school but studying
Monuments of its own magnificence;
And therefore I have sailed the seas and come
To the holy city of Byzantium.

3

O sages standing in God's holy fire
As in the gold mosaic of a wall,
Come from the holy fire, perne in a gyre,
And be the singing-masters of my soul.
Consume my heart away; sick with desire
And fastened to a dying animal
It knows not what it is; and gather me
Into the artifice of eternity.

4

Once out of nature I shall never take
My bodily form from any natural thing,
But such a form as Grecian goldsmiths make
Of hammered gold and gold enameling
To keep a drowsy Emperor awake;
Or set upon a golden bough to sing
To lords and ladies of Byzantium
Of what is past, or passing, or to come.

—*William Butler Yeats*

INTERPRETATION OF
"SAILING TO BYZANTIUM"

Start with the Title

A convenient place to start is the title. According to the dictionary, Byzantium was an ancient Greek city on the Bosporus and the Sea of Marmara. Its buildings were characterized by a highly formal structure and the use of rich color. However, this doesn't tell us why Yeats selected this particular empire; there were, after all, many other ancient cities noted for the same qualities. Looking through other poems by the same author as well as critical studies of his work, we find that Byzantium had become for Yeats the symbol for art or artifice as contrasted to the natural world of biological activity. As Yeats matured, he turned away from the sensual world of growth and constant change to the world of art. Later, though, he would return to the sensual world. As he wrote in his work *A Vision*, "I think that if I could be given a month of antiquity and leave to spend it anywhere I chose, I would spend it in Byzantium [what we today call Istanbul] a little before Justinian opened St. Sophia and closed the Academy of Plato [around 535 A.D.].... I think that in early Byzantium ... religious, aesthetic, and practical life were one, that architects and artificers ... spoke to the multitude in gold and silver." In his old age, the poet rejected the world of growth and death—biological change—to turn instead to structures of what he called "unaging intellect."

Look at the First Line and First Stanza

This discussion fits with the opening line reference to "old men," which we also could have discovered by looking up Yeats's age when he wrote this poem and the date of the poem itself. Yeats lived from 1865 to 1939, and this poem was published in 1927, when the poet was sixty-two years old. Thus, we can also infer that the poem has some autobiographical leanings.

The entire first stanza discusses the natural world of biological activity, the endless process of creatures being "begotten, born," and dying. The speaker is an old man, he states, turning away from all this.

Study the Second Stanza

The second stanza continues with the theme of the aging man, here made into a brilliant and oft-quoted symbol of the "tattered coat upon a stick." And so, seeking the unchanging world of art, the speaker comes, symbolically, to all that Byzantium has come to represent.

Move on to the Third Stanza

The "gold mosaic" in the third stanza refers to mosaic figures on the walls of the Church of the Hagia Sophia ("Holy Wisdom") in Byzantium. There are two words that must be explained in this stanza. The first is "perne," which means a bobbin, reel, or spool, and can also be spelled "pirn." The second is "gyre," which means to whirl around in a spiral motion. This had become one of Yeats's favorite words, which he used as a verb, meaning "to spin around." He associated this spinning with the spinning of fate. Here he is asking the saints on the wall to descend and enter into this symbolic spinning motion, and thus help *him* enter into their state of being. We see this in the final line of the stanza, "… and gather me/Into the artifice of eternity."

Conclude with the Final Stanza

Once he is able to leave the natural flux, he says in the final stanza, he shall not again assume a natural shape. Rather, he will assume the form that Grecian workers of old might fashion. The form is specifically that of a bird. His notes say that he had read somewhere that "in the Emperor's palace in Byzantium was a tree made of gold and silver and artificial birds that sang."

Therefore, we can conclude that "gyre" and "Byzantium" are key words in this poem, and their special meanings shed light on his feelings about life, art, and approaching old age. In this poem he is turning away from the natural world to embrace the timeless world of art, represented for him in the symbol of Byzantium.

Let's take a look at another of Yeats's most famous poems, *Among School Children*. As you read through this poem, apply the techniques of analysis you just learned. Study the title, punctuation, pacing, and symbols for clues to interpretation.

Among School Children

1

I walk through the long schoolroom questioning;
A kind old nun in a white hood replies;
The children learn to cipher and to sing,
To study reading-books and history,
To cut and sew, to be neat in everything
In the best modern way—the children's eyes
In momentary wonder stare upon
A sixty-year-old smiling public man.

2

I dream of a Ledaean body, bent
Above a sinking fire, a tale that she
Told of harsh reproof, or trivial event
That changed some childish day to tragedy—
Told, and it seemed that our two natures blent
Into a sphere from youthful sympathy,
Or else, to alter Plato's parable,
Into the yolk and white of the one shell.

3

And thinking of that fit of grief or rage
I look upon one child or t'other there
And wonder if she stood so at that age—
For even daughters of the swan can share
Something of every paddler's heritage—
And had that colour upon cheek or hair,
And thereupon my heart is driven wild:
She stands before me as a living child.

4

The present image floats into the mind—
Did Quattrocento finger fashion it
Hollow of cheek as though it drank the wind
And took a mess of shadows for its meat?
And I though never of Ledaean kind
Had pretty plumage once—enough of that,
Better to smile on all that smile, and show
There is a comfortable kind of old scarecrow.

5

What youthful mother, a shape upon her lap
Honey of generation had betrayed,
And that must sleep, shriek, struggle to escape
As recollection or the drug decide,
Would think her son, did she but see that shape
With sixty or more winters on its head,
A compensation for the pang of his birth,
Or the uncertainty of his setting forth?

6

Plato thought nature but a spume that plays
Upon a ghostly paradigm of things;
Solider Aristotle played the taws
Upon the bottom of a king of kings;
World-famous golden-thighed Pythagoras
Fingered upon a fiddle-stick or strings
What a star sang and careless Muses heard:
Old clothes upon old sticks to scare a bird.

7

Both nuns and mothers worship images,
But those the candles light as not as those
That animate a mother's reveries,
But keep a marble or a bronze repose.
And yet they too break hearts—O Presences
That passion, piety or affection knows,
And that all heavenly glory symbolise—
O self-born mockers of man's enterprise;

8

Labour is blossoming or dancing where
The body is not bruised to pleasure soul,
Nor beauty born out of its own despair,
Nor blear-eyed wisdom out of midnight oil.
O chestnut tree, great-rooted blossomer,
Are you the leaf, the blossom, or the bole?
O body swayed to music, O brightening glance,
How can we know the dancer from the dance?

—*William Butler Yeats*

INTERPRETATION OF
"AMONG SCHOOL CHILDREN"

Read the poem using the same techniques you learned as you read "Sailing to Byzantium." Since this poem is also by Yeats, you can see how a poet's body of work often functions as a unified whole. The more examples of a poet's art you read, the more you will understand the symbols and allusions the artist employs.

Look at the First Line and First Stanza
The first stanza tells us that the speaker, a "sixty-year-old smiling public man," is touring a parochial school (note the reference to a nun), asking what the children are learning. Again, we can infer from this information that the speaker bears some relation to Yeats, as we check the

dates and discover that he was indeed in his early sixties when he wrote this poem. A quick look at his biography reveals that he was very well known and well respected at this time.

Study the Second Stanza

The second stanza contains many difficult *allusions*, or references. Let's take them one at a time. First, Zeus visited Leda in the form of a swan. As a result of the union, Leda gave birth to Helen of Troy. Yeats saw Zeus's visit as an "annunciation marking the beginning of Greek civilization." In Yeats's private mythology, this is used as a reference to Maud Gonne, a woman he very much admired. She functions in his verse as a kind of Helen, a shining ideal of womanhood—and betrayal. The first two lines of the stanza refer to Aristophanes' explanation of Love in Plato's *Symposium*. Aristophanes suggested that primeval man was round with four hands and four feet, backs and sides forming a circle, one head having two faces. After the division, the two parts of man, each desiring the other half, throw their arms around each other in an embrace, not wanting to be alone. As the daughter of Leda and the swan, Helen would have been born from an egg, and this suggests Yeats's image of the coming together. This stanza, then, can be seen as describing the child telling the speaker some tale that changed their normally happy and carefree childhood day to tragedy (as it would seem to a child). After they shared the sadness of the event, they were in such sympathy and agreement with each other that their very natures blent into the form of a single being. Thus, the image suggests how two persons can share grief and blend into one when their natures are in accord.

Move on to the Third Stanza

Suddenly back in the present again, the speaker wonders if any of the little girls before him looks as Maud did all those years ago when they were children together. In this third stanza, he suddenly sees a little girl who looks just as Maud did, many years ago, and his "heart is driven wild."

Analyze the Fourth Stanza

In the fourth stanza, the speaker thinks about how Maud looks in the present, as a mature woman. Quattrocento is a reference to the fifteenth century, and here he is calling to mind the painters of the period, especially Botticelli, noted for his lovely portraits of women. The speaker notes that although he was never as handsome as she was beautiful, he did have "pretty plumage once." He stops his remembrances then, for that is all passed now, and it is better to smile about the past for the sake of all the schoolchildren looking at the famous visitor. He now sees himself as "a comfortable kind of old scarecrow," smiling nicely for the children.

Infer Meaning from the Fifth Stanza

In this stanza he thinks of his mother, looking at her infant son now sixty years old. The references here are complex. The phrase "honey of generation" was taken from Porphyry's essay, Yeats tells us, but Porphyry did not consider it a "drug" that destroys the memory of prebirth freedom. Porphyry was a philosopher who wrote during the third century A.D. By erasing the memory of happiness before birth, "honey of generation" "betray[s]" an infant into being born into the world. The infant will either "sleep" or "struggle" to escape from the world, depending on whether the drug works or the memory of the bliss of life before birth takes over. Would his mother, looking at her sixty-year-old son, think that his present "shape" (i.e., condition, status, fame) was compensation for the pain of his birth or her fear of what fate would allot to him?

Connect Meaning in the Sixth Stanza

In the sixth stanza, we see that Plato believed that nature was but an appearance ("spume") covering the final spiritual and mathematical reality ("ghostly paradigm"). Aristotle was Alexander the Great's tutor and beat him by using "taws" or straps. Aristotle believed that form was really in the matter of nature and thus nature itself had reality. So the first two lines here explain what Plato thought about nature, and the second two tell us that Aristotle disciplined Alexander (the king of kings) with a strap. Pythagoras was a Greek philosopher who lived during the sixth century B.C. and was interested in mathematics and music. His followers, called Pythagoreans, developed a mathematical philosophy of numerical relationships and tied together the fields of mathematics and astronomy in a theory of the music of the spheres. These followers regarded their master as a god with a golden thigh. Thus, these three lines refer to Pythagoras and his followers. The final line of this stanza is a contemptuous description of all three philosophers.

Turn to the Seventh Stanza

The beginning of this stanza says that both nuns and mothers worship images: Nuns worship images of Christ or the Virgin; mothers worship their own inward images of their children. Mothers do not worship the same images nuns do, as the next line states.

Conclude with the Final Stanza

The final stanza draws together all the images and expresses Yeats's theme: Life is a cosmic dance in which every human ability and part joins smoothly. The individual becomes part of the whole, as the dancer becomes one with the dance. He sees this cosmic dance as a means of bringing together the conflicting parts of past and present and daily life. This concluding image has become very famous.

Chapter 2

A Brief History of Meter

From the very first poems, oral accounts of adventures we date from the eighth century, an individual line of poetry has been the basic unit we recognize as poetic. Up until the time of Walt Whitman's revolutionary poetic experiments, we were even able to say that a poem "looked like a poem," by which we meant that the lines stood apart in a certain recognizable manner and did not run together like prose paragraphs. The act of breaking down poetic lines to their basic units to discover their rhyme and rhythm is called *scansion*. *Scanning* a poem is not an attempt to discover its meaning, as we did in the previous section of this book; rather, it is breaking down the verse into its textual parts. When we scan a poem, we will discover that there are four basic types of verse: *accentual, syllabic, accentual-syllabic*, and *free verse*.

ACCENTUAL VERSE

The earliest recorded poetry, the eighth-century Anglo-Saxon verse mentioned above, was measured neither by rhyme nor by meter. From its inception in other languages, English has been an *accented* language. This means that certain words receive more spoken emphasis than others, that we stress certain parts or sounds within the word. The Anglo-Saxon poets used this system of accents as the basis of their poetry. The accents determined the length of the line of poetry. We use this system to indicate accents:

An *ictus* (´) over a syllable means that it is to be accented.
A *breve* (˘) over a syllable means that it is *not* accented.

If we look at a few sample lines from the Old English poem *Beowulf,*
we can see how the accentual system works to determine meaning:

Hwǽt! Wē Gár-Dena   in geár-dagum,
þēod-cýninga,   þrym gefrúnon,
hū ðā æþelingas   éllen frémedon!

The first line has nine syllables; the second, ten; the third, ten or eleven.
But the number of syllables per line doesn't matter in verse that is being
scanned by accent. What is important is that each line has the same
number of accents. As you go through the poem, you will discover that
four accents predominate per line. No matter how you read the lines,
though, no one would stress words such as "the" and "to."

Sprung Rhythm

Accentual verse comes up again in the works of noted poet Gerard
Manley Hopkins, mentioned previously. Hopkins, who lived from 1844
to 1889, reintroduced accented verse to the modern ear with a variation he called *sprung rhythm,* in which strongly accented syllables are
pushed up against unaccented ones to produce a new way of scanning
verse. Hopkins hoped to shake up readers to his meaning by forcing
them to look at his words in a new light.

SYLLABIC VERSE

History of Syllabic Verse

Syllabic verse has a basis different from that of accented verse. The French
language, unlike English, makes little use of strongly accented words.
One rarely counts out the number of accents in a line of French verse.
Instead, the French developed a way of counting the number of syllables to establish the length of the lines of verse. When William the
Conqueror invaded England in 1066, he introduced French poets experienced in syllabic rhythms and rhyme. The next few centuries, until

the 1400s, saw the change from Old English (*Beowulf,* as we saw before, for example) to Middle English. Old English and French melded together; the language of the lower classes and the language of the court meshed to form Middle English, a midpoint between Old English and modern English. For a short time, the English court spoke French and listened to French poets composing verse within the strict confines of a syllabic line. Although this was a brief period and syllabic verse was altered quickly into accentual-syllabic poetry, later poets occasionally utilized lines determined solely by the number of syllables. In these verses, the number of accents could vary as long as the number of syllables remained constant.

Modern Experiments
Modern poets continue to experiment with the syllabic idea, for it enables the poet to escape the boundaries of a more regulated and often jingling or monotonous rhythmic cadence. Dylan Thomas, the Welsh poet who lived from 1914 to 1953, constructed such syllabic verse, as this sample shows:

> In my craft or sullen art
> Exercised in the still night
> When only the moon rages
> And the lovers lie abed ...

Each line has seven syllables, even though the accents change in each line, both in their number and position.

ACCENTUAL-SYLLABIC VERSE

Accentual-syllabic verse is the kind of poetry most people would recognize immediately as "poetry." It often rhymes, has a definite beat—called *meter*—and usually moves with a predictable regularity. From the fourteenth century to the present, accentual-syllabic verse has been the norm, following a strict system of rules. In some instances, the skill of the poet has been equated with his or her ability to follow these "rules" and to manipulate the words within their confines.

History of Accentual-Syllabic Verse

Accentual-syllabic verse came into being when the counting of accents and the counting of syllables in a line occurred at the same time. Although many modern poets feel that this kind of verse sounds forced and artificial, for centuries few were bothered by this at all. Rather, they felt that such writing was lovely and truly "poetic"—the measure of the poet's skill in forging words and ideas into a preconceived pattern. Poetry was closely linked to music and was understood to be little more than the construction of a series of sounds, a work of skill and art. Conventional verse gains much of its success and beauty from the fact that English is a language in which word order is highly significant. When the poet is able to fashion language into a verse that moves with ease, a tension and power are created. It is like a formal garden, trained under the craftsman's eye for symmetry and order. Nature has been subdued, brought under human control, and the work that results has a structure that many find enormously pleasing.

The Foot

The *foot* of English poetry was created by counting out the number of accents and syllables together. Because English has an accented base, dividing a line into stressed and unstressed syllables creates certain recurring patterns. These measures also fit the pattern of classical Greek and Latin. In counting stresses, the two classical languages were also counting duration—the length of time it took to express an idea. In Greek and Latin, syllables were separated according to length, not stress. Long and short syllables were equated to what English terms stressed or unstressed, the *quality* of a syllable. Therefore, counting in accentual-syllabic verse came to be measured in *feet*.

Types of Metric Feet

A foot is composed of either two or three syllables, such that the nature of the foot is determined by the placement of the accent. Every English sentence, no matter whether classified as poetry or prose (non-poetry), is made up of these units. The placement determines the *rhythm* of the line. Even more significantly, feet establish the *meter* of a line, the regularity of a verse in an accentual-syllabic piece. One particular foot determines the poem's rhythm. A slash (/) is used to divide the feet in a line.

There are six basic types of metrical feet in English verse:

Common feet:

iamb	˘ ´	unstressed, stressed syllables
anapest	˘ ˘ ´	2 unstressed, 1 stressed syllable
trochee	´ ˘	stressed, unstressed syllables
dactyl	´ ˘ ˘	1 stressed, 2 unstressed syllables

Less common feet:

spondee	´ ´	2 stressed syllables
phyrrhic	˘ ˘	2 unstressed syllables

Here are examples of each:

Iamb	Ĭ táste/ ă líq/ uŏr név/ĕr bréwed
Trochee	Eárth, rĕ/ céive aň/ hoňorĕd/ guést
Anapest	T˘e Ašsyŕ/iaň caňe do˙wn/ likĕ t˘e wólf/ oň t˘e fóld
Dactyl	Oút ŏf t˘e/ crádlĕ/ eńdlešslў/ roćkiňg

Scanning Lines

But poetic lines are not usually composed of only one type of metrical foot, for this would sound dull. Variations are constructed to give the line more exciting movement. In lines with mixed feet, whichever foot is most prevalent determines the type and name of the line. Thus, a line with six iambs and four trochees would be called an iambic line.

After we figure out the predominant foot in a line, we mark the accents and count the number of feet in order to determine the total length of the line. For example:

Ĭ táste/ ă líq/ uŏr név/ĕr bréwed

has a total of four iambic feet. This is called *iambic tetrameter.* The following chart explains the number of feet and the length of the line:

Number of Feet	Line Length
one	monometer
two	dimeter
three	trimeter
four	tetrameter
five	pentameter
six	hexameter
seven	heptameter

While it is possible to have a line containing more than seven feet, in actual practice, the heptameter line—a line from 14 to 21 syllables long—approaches the outer limits of most poems.

Iambic Pentameter: The Most Common English Poetic Line

The most common foot in English is the *iamb*, perhaps because the use of articles—the, a, an—establishes that an unstressed syllable will occur before a stressed one. Children's verse, such as nursery rhymes, often has trochees dominating. This may be because children do not use as many articles in speech as do adults. The most common line in English poetry is the iambic pentameter line, in part because a line of more than ten syllables requires an intake of breath, which translates as requiring another line.

Elision

Even though the measurement of an accentual-syllabic line can be very precise, as illustrated earlier, there is a way for the poet to lengthen or to shorten the line, even within strict metrical lines. This method is called *elision*. For example, two vowels placed side by side may become a single syllable. We consider the letters *h*, *w*, and *v* as vowels, as well as the more easily recognized *a*, *e*, *i*, *o*, and *u*. The following four lines by the poet Sir Walter Raleigh illustrate the process:

> The flowers do fade, and wanton fields
> To wayward winter reckoning yields;

> A honey tongue, a heart of gall,
> Is fancy's spring, but sorrow's fall.

This excerpt, part of the poem "The Nymph's Reply to the Shepherd," is written in iambic tetrameter, which means that it should have eight syllables per line. The first two lines, however, count out to nine syllables apiece, while the second two come out to the expected eight. We deal with the extra syllable in the first line by taking the word "flowers" and treating it differently. The vowels *o, w,* and *e* come together to create what we call a *diphthong,* meaning that the two syllables may be counted or pronounced as one if the poet should so desire. The same is done with the word "reckoning" in the second line, compressing into two syllables what might have been considered three with more formal pronunciation. The same process can be seen in Milton's sonnet "On the Late Massacre in Piedmont," which has an iambic pentameter line with eleven syllables instead of the usual ten:

> ... and they
> To heaven. Their martyred blood and ashes sow
> O'er all th'Italian fields, where still doth sway
> The triple tyrant ...

Elision occurs here with the words "To Heaven" where the two-syllable word "Heaven" is treated as though it had only one syllable. In the next line, "Over" is written "O'er," indicating elision by spelling. In the same manner, "the Italian fields" is shortened to "th'Italian fields." It is rare today to find words contracted as Milton did to show the elision, for the style is felt to be old-fashioned, but elision is nonetheless present in modern accentual-syllabic verse. You will be able to find it when you read lines for their meter.

Masculine and Feminine Endings

Accents may also be used to give the poet greater leeway at the end of a line of verse. A line is said to have a *feminine ending* when it ends on an unaccented syllable and a *masculine ending* when it ends on an accented one. The following lines from Milton's epic *Paradise Lost* have a feminine ending:

> Thus they in mutual accusation spent
> The fruitless hours, but neither self-condemning;

The second line has an extra syllable because of its feminine ending, but as an unaccented syllable at the close of a line, the "ing" may be discounted. Thus a line that counts out to eleven syllables may, at the poet's discretion, become technically a ten-syllable line thanks to the feminine ending.

FREE VERSE

Free verse has no fixed metrical pattern: it is free from counting, measuring, meter. Free verse replaced the expected pattern of a particular foot with a looser movement called *rhythm*. Free verse shares a common basis with accentual and syllabic verse, but it must be devoid of all predominate measurements to be considered truly "free." The placement of accents must follow no set pattern; the syllables must not be able to be measured with any regularity. In the same manner, *rhyme*, if it is used at all, is irregular. A poem may be considered free verse if you can find no accentual or syllabic pattern. It may, of course, have other regularities. This type of verse can be found in the work of E.E. Cummings and Walt Whitman, among others.

There are some modern poets who consider free verse to be anything in which no attempt has been made to make the lines of verse fit a definite pattern, even though they do, in fact, have patterns at intervals. Often a page of poetry will look like free verse but, upon closer examination, will reveal itself to be syllabic or accentual. The poems of T.S. Eliot and Dylan Thomas are of this type. There are many other modern poems that have no metric regularity and are thus considered free verse, although they have a great deal of rhythm, such as the work of Lawrence Ferlinghetti.

Concrete Poems

Some poets have carried matters to such a length that they have created poems where the shape, not the words, is what matters. These are called *concrete poems*. These poems leave it to the reader's eye to create a pleasing or important shape and meaning.

Stanzas

We have thus far looked at rhythm and accents, syllables and lines, but it is obvious that these can be grouped in several ways. Often these lines arrange themselves into blocks of specific numbers—two lines, four lines, six lines, etc. Usually there is a space, followed by an equal grouping of lines. A grouping of lines is called a *stanza,* roughly the same as a paragraph in a prose work. Stanzas may be classified as follows:

Types of Stanzas

couplets	2-line stanzas
quatrains	4-line stanzas
sextets	6-line stanzas
octets	8-line stanzas

REVIEW OF METER

accent   The act of emphasizing or stressing certain words or parts of words.

accentual verse   A system of verse in which accents are used to determine the length of lines of poetry. The number of syllables per line is not important. This type of verse is found mainly in the works of the earliest poets, dating from the eighth century.

accentual-syllabic verse   A type of verse in which the counting of accents and syllables occurs within the same line. It is the type of poetry most people instantly recognize as "poetic," for it has a definite beat and often rhymes.

breve   The ˘ mark over a syllable to indicate that it is not accented.

concrete verse   Poems shaped like the specific objects they describe.

diphthong   Two syllables that are counted and pronounced as one, used in poetry to make the words fit the metrical requirements.

elision   The elimination of a vowel, consonant, or syllable in pronunciation. It usually occurs in verse at the end of a word when the next word begins with a vowel and is used to shorten or lengthen a line to make it fit metrical requirements.

feminine ending   A line that ends on an unaccented syllable.

foot/feet   A group of stressed and unstressed syllables combining to form a unit of verse.

foot	scansion	definition
iamb	˘ ´	unstressed, stressed syllables
trochee	´ ˘	stressed, unstressed syllables
anapest	˘ ˘ ´	2 unstressed, 1 stressed syllable
dactyl	´ ˘ ˘	1 stressed, 2 unstressed syllables
spondee	´ ´	2 stressed syllables
phyrrhic	˘ ˘	2 unstressed syllables

Number of Feet	Line Length
one	monometer
two	dimeter
three	trimeter
four	tetrameter
five	pentameter
six	hexameter
seven	heptameter

free verse   Poetry without a fixed metrical pattern. The rhythmical lines vary in length and are usually unrhymed. Although the form may appear unrestrained, there is a firm pattern to the words.

ictus   The ´ mark over a syllable to indicate that it is accented.

masculine ending   A line that ends on an accented syllable.

meter   The "beat" of a line of verse determined by the kind and number of poetic feet.

scansion   The act of breaking down lines into their basic units to discover rhythm and meter.

sprung rhythm   The reintroduction of accentual verse in the works of Gerard Manley Hopkins (1844–1889) in which strongly accented syllables are pushed up against unaccented ones to produce greater tension and emphasis within the verse.

stanza   An arrangement of a certain number of lines forming the divisions of a poem.

syllabic verse   A system of verse in which syllables are used to determine the length of a line of poetry. This type of verse flourished mainly in the period between 1066 and 1400, although modern poets have experimented with it.

types of stanzas

couplets	2-line stanzas
quatrains	4-line stanzas
sextets	6-line stanzas
octets	8-line stanzas

Chapter 3

Rhyme and Figurative Language

Rhyme is the repetition of the same or similar sounds often occurring at set intervals in a poem. For example, the word "light" rhymes with "fight," "sight," and so on. The rhyming consonant is the sound "ight," on which the poet forms other rhymes by changing the first letter or letters. Many people find rhyme pleasing in itself, but it also serves to suggest order and pattern to a poem. In addition, rhyme often relates to the meaning of the verse, for it brings words together and suggests relationships.

To some extent, the use of rhyme is similar to the musical pattern of returning to a recognized theme or note. In ancient poetry, before the advent of writing, rhyme was invaluable, for it was far easier to commit to memory a poem that had a strong pattern of rhyme.

KINDS OF RHYME

Alliteration
Alliteration is the repetition of an initial sound in two or more words. Also called *internal rhyme,* it is not technically considered a type of rhyme, but it will be treated in this section because it adds to the musical quality of a poem. Here is an example of alliteration:

> About the lilting house and happy as the grass was green

This phrase shows alliteration in the repetition of the *h* in "house" and "happy" and the *gr* in "grass" and "green." In Macbeth's line: "after life's fitful fever," true alliteration is found in the repeated *f*'s of "fitful fever" and hidden alliteration in the *f*'s of "after," "life's," and "fitful." Accentual Anglo-Saxon poetry used alliteration a great deal to create the balance and music of its verse.

Assonance
Assonance occurs when the vowels in the word are the same, but the consonants are not. Assonance is a variation of half-rhyme. We see assonance in the words "seat" and "weak" and "tide" and "mine."

Consonance
Consonance occurs when the consonants are the same but the vowels do not match, as in the words "luck" and "lick." Consonance, like assonance, is a variation of half-rhyme.

Euphony and Cacophony
Euphony is the use of pleasant-sounding or harmonious combinations of words, while *cacophony* is harsh or discordant sound used to produce an inharmonious effect.

Eye-rhyme
Eye-rhyme occurs when words are spelled the same and look alike but have a different sound. This can be seen in lines 3 and 4 of Sir Walter Raleigh's poem "The Nymph's Reply to the Shepherd":

> These pretty pleasures might me move
> To live with thee and be thy love

The words "move" and "love" are examples of eye-rhyme. These rhymes are also called *historical rhymes* as the pronunciation has changed over the years.

Half-rhyme
Half-rhyme is also called *slant rhyme, approximate rhyme, near rhyme,* and *off rhyme*. It occurs when there are changes within the vowel sounds

of words intended to rhyme and only the final consonant sounds of the words are identical. The stressed vowel sounds as well as the initial consonant sounds (if any) differ. Here are some examples:

soul: oil   firth: forth   trolley: bully

The following lines from William Whitehead's "Je Ne Sais Quois" exemplify half-rhyme:

> Tis not her face that love creates,
>   For there no grace revel;
> Tis not her shape, for there the Fates
>   Had rather been uncivil.

"Revel" and "uncivil" in lines 2 and 4 illustrate half-rhyme because the vowel sound changes, but the "vl" sound remains the same.

Internal Rhyme
Internal rhyme occurs within the line instead of at the end. Oscar Wilde's "Each narrow cell within which we dwell" is an example of internal rhyme because the words "cell" and "dwell" rhyme.

Masculine and Feminine Rhymes
Masculine and *feminine rhymes* are the equivalent of masculine and feminine line endings. Rhymes that end on a stress, such as "van" and "span," are masculine, while those ending on an unstressed syllable, such as "falling" and "calling," are considered feminine. Thus, "stark/mark" and "support/retort" would be masculine, while "revival/arrival" and "flatter/batter" are feminine. Feminine rhyme is also called *double rhyme.* Also a feminine rhyme, triple rhyme is defined in *A Handbook to Literature**** as "a rhyme in which the correspondence of sound lies in three consecutive syllables." "Machinery/scenery" and "tenderly/slenderly" are two examples.

---

*(William Flint Thrall and Addison Hibbard, *A Handbook to Literature*, ed. Hugh Holman. New York: The Odyssey Press, 1960, p. 495.)

True or Perfect Rhyme

True or *perfect rhyme* occurs when the first consonants change, but the following consonants or vowels stay the same. This can also be referred to as *exact rhyme*. Perfect rhyme involves identical sounds, not identical spellings. For example, "fix" and "sticks," like "buffer" and "rougher," though spelled differently, are all perfect rhymes. Anne Bradstreet's poem "Before the Birth of One of Her Children," written in 1678, illustrates true rhyme:

> All things within this fading world hath end,
> Adversity doth still our joys attend;
> No ties so strong, no friends so dear and sweet,
> But with death's parting blow is sure to meet.

To show *end rhyme* (rhyme that appears at the end of a line), words are labeled with letters. In the lines quoted, "end" rhymes with "attend," so both will be labeled *a*. "Sweet" rhymes with "meet," so both will be labeled *b*. This pattern of true rhyme creates what is called a *rhyme scheme*. Here, the rhyme scheme is *aabb*.

FIGURATIVE LANGUAGE

Robert Frost, one of the most famous twentieth-century poets, once said, "Poetry provides the one permissible way of saying one thing and meaning another." Of course, this is an exaggeration, but it does underline the importance of *figurative language*—saying one thing in terms of another. Words have a literal meaning that can be looked up in any dictionary, but they can also be employed so that something other than that literal dictionary meaning is intended. What is impossible or difficult to convey to a reader through the literal use of language may be highly possible through the use of *figures of speech*, also called *tropes*. Figures of speech make language significant, moving, and fascinating. "My love is a rose" is, when taken at face value, ridiculous, for few people love a plant with a prickly, thorny stem. But "rose" suggests many other possible interpretations—delicate beauty, something soft and rare, a costly item, etc.—and so it can be implied in a figurative sense to mean "love" or "loved one."

If a reader comes across the phrase "Brutus growled," the reader is forced, if the poem has indicated that Brutus is human, to accept "growled" in a non-literal manner. We understand that it is likely that the poet is suggesting that Brutus sounded like an animal, perhaps a lion or a bear, and indicates Brutus's irritation or unrest. The author calls forth the suggestion of wild animals to describe Brutus most vividly and accurately. This is far more effective than saying "Brutus spoke roughly" or "Brutus acted like a loud person." By using a vivid figure of speech, the author calls the reader's imagination into play.

THE FIGURES OF SPEECH

Allegory

Allegory occurs when one idea or object is represented in the shape of another. In medieval morality plays and in some poems, abstract ideas such as virtues and vices appear as people. In this way the reader can understand a moral or a lesson more easily. In Emily Dickinson's poem "Because I Could Not Stop for Death," death appears as the allegorical figure of a coachman, kindly stopping to pick up the speaker after her death on the road to eternity. Here is the first stanza of the poem:

> Because I could not stop for Death—
> He kindly stopped for me—
> The Carriage held just but Ourselves—
> And Immortality.

Ambiguity

Ambiguity allows multiple meanings to coexist in a word or a metaphor. It does not mean that the word or term is unclear; rather, it means that the perceptive reader can see more than one possible interpretation at the same time. Puns, for example, offer ambiguity, as these lines from Wyatt's "They Flee from Me" show: "But since that I so kindly (*sic*) am servéd/I fain would know what she hath deservéd." The word "kindely" means both "served by a group" and "courteously."

Apostrophe

Apostrophe is closely related to personification (see pages 35–36). Here, a thing is addressed directly, as though it were a person listening to the conversation. For example, we have Wordsworth's "Milton! thou should'st be living at this hour," although Milton had obviously died. Apostrophe and personification go hand in hand in Donne's "Busy old fool, unruly Sun," and Wyatt's "My lute, awake." Milton's apostrophe has only a hint of laurels as listening things in "Yet once more, O ye laurels."

Conceit

A *conceit* is a metaphor that goes beyond the original vehicle to other tenors and vehicles. In "A Valediction Forbidding Mourning" by John Donne, the souls of the two lovers become the same as the two legs of a draftsman's compass:

> If they be two, they are two so
>   As stiff twin compasses are two;
> Thy soul, the fixed foot, makes no show
>   To move, but doth, if th' other do.
>
> And though it in the center sit,
>   Yet when the other far doth roam,
> It leans and hearkens after it,
>   And grows erect, as that comes home.

Connotation and Denotation

Connotation is the generally accepted meaning(s) of a word, in contrast to *denotation*, which is the dictionary meaning of a word. Connotation adds additional richness to the meaning of a word, and by extension, to the meaning of a poem. In the line, "She was the sickle; I, poor I, the rake," the word "rake" has a clear denotation—a gardening tool designed to pick up clippings from a lawn or a garden that a sickle might have cut down. In the context of the poem, however, the word "rake" has the connotation of a debauched man. The denotation and connotation work together to give the poem greater depth and further the author's theme.

Contrast
Contrast shows the difference between two objects. In this sense it is the opposite of *comparison,* which shows similarities. In the following example by Shakespeare, we see his mistress contrasted to various accepted symbols of adoration:

> My mistress' eyes are nothing like the sun;
> Coral is far more red than her lips' red;
> If snow be white, why then her breasts are dun;
> If hairs be wires, black wires grow on her head.

Dead Metaphor
A metaphor that has lost its figurative value through overuse is called a dead metaphor. "Eye of a needle" and "foot of a hill" are examples.

Dramatic Irony, Sophoclean Irony, Tragic Irony
Here the irony refers to conditions or affairs that are the tragic reverse of what the participants have expected. Thus, irony occurs when Eve eats the forbidden fruit because she is faced with great sorrow when she had expected great joy. Macbeth (from Shakespeare's tragedy *Macbeth*) expects great happiness to follow his killing King Duncan; instead, he finds that by his deed he forfeits all that makes life worth living. King Oedipus accuses the blind prophet of corruption, but by the end of the play he learns, as the audience has realized all along, that he is himself corrupt, that he has been blind to what is real, and that the prophet's visions were indeed correct. As in verbal irony, dramatic irony is marked by contrast, but here it is not between what the speaker says and means, but between what the speaker says and means and the real state of affairs.

Extended Metaphor

An *extended metaphor* results when a metaphor becomes elaborate or complex. It has length and the ideas are more fully illustrated.

Hyperbole or Overstatement

This is *exaggeration* for a specific literary effect. Shakespeare's Sonnet 97 contains an example:

> How like a winter hath my absence been
> From thee, the pleasure of the fleeting year!
> What freezings have I felt, what dark days seen!
> What old December's bareness everywhere!

We realize that Shakespeare did not literally freeze with real cold when he was parted from his loved one. We also realize that the day did not turn dark nor June turn to December; rather, he is saying this to illustrate the depth of his despair at their separation. The same process can be seen at work in this phrase from a poem by Lovelace: "When I lie tangled in her hair/And fetter'd to her eye...." Obviously, he is not captured in her hair nor chained to her eye; what he is suggesting, however, is that he is a prisoner to her beauty and finds himself unable to escape its spell.

Implicit or Submerged Metaphor

If both terms of the metaphor are not present ("My winged heart" instead of "My heart is a bird") we have what is called a *submerged metaphor*.

Invocation

Invocation is an address to a god or muse whose aid is sought. This is commonly found at the beginning of an epic, as in Milton's "Sing, Heavenly Muse" at the opening of *Paradise Lost*.

Irony

Irony states one thing in one tone of voice when, in fact, the opposite meaning is intended. Auden's "The Unknown Citizen," for example, ends ironically by making a statement that the reader knows is false. As a matter of fact, the entire poem is ironic in that it condemns the State by using the State's own terms of praise:

> Was he free? Was he happy? The question is absurd;
> Had anything been wrong, we should certainly have heard.

Irony of Fate or Cosmic Irony

This term describes the view that God, Fate, or some supernatural being is amused to manipulate human beings as a puppeteer would manipulate puppets. For example, it would be an irony of fate that a prisoner receives his pardon right after his execution.

Litotes

Litotes is a special form of understatement. It affirms something by negating the opposite. For example, "He's no fool" means that he is very shrewd.

Metaphor

A *metaphor* is a comparison without the words *like* or *as*. Once established, this relationship between unlike objects alters our perception of both. In the most basic metaphor, such as "My love is a rose," "rose" and "love" are equated. They are not alike, but they interact with each other, so the abstract word "love" becomes concrete. Now it is not a vague internal emotion but an object that could be picked and caressed. We can make the comparison even more specific by describing the rose in more detail—color, variety, and so forth. The subject of the comparison—in this case, love—is called the *tenor*, and the figure that completes the metaphor—the rose—the *vehicle*. These terms were coined by critic I.A. Richards. In the following metaphor by John Donne, the poet's doctors become the map-makers of the heavens, while the poet's body becomes the map in which the ultimate destiny of his soul can be divined:

> Whilst my physicians by their love are grown
>   Cosmographers, and I their map, who lie
> Flat on this bed ...

Metonymy

Metonymy is the substitution of one item for another item that it suggests or to which it is closely related. For example, if a letter is said to be in Milton's own "hand," it means that the letter is in Milton's own handwriting. As another example, Sidney wrote in "Astrophil and Stella": "What, may it be that even in heavenly place/ That busy archer his sharp arrows tries?" "That busy archer" is a reference to Cupid, the god of love frequently depicted as a cherubic little boy with a quiver full of arrows. Here he is at his usual occupation—shooting arrows into the hearts of unsuspecting men and women. Thus the poet, by relating an archer to love, describes love without specifically using the word.

Mixed Metaphor

A *mixed metaphor* combines two metaphors, often with absurd results. For example, "Let's iron out the bottlenecks," is silly, for it is an obvious impossibility.

Onomatopoeia

Onomatopoeia occurs when the sound of a word echoes or suggests the meaning of the word. "Hiss" and "buzz" are examples. There is a tendency for readers to see onomatopoeia in far too many instances, in words such as "thunder" and "horror." Many words that are thought to echo the sounds they suggest merely contain sounds that seem to have a resemblance to the things they suggest. Tennyson's lines from "Come Down, O Maid" are often cited to show true onomatopoeia:

> The moan of doves in immemorial elms
> And murmuring of innumerable bees.

This suggests the sound of birds and bees among old trees.

Oxymoron

Oxymoron is the combination of contradictory or incongruous terms. "Living death," "mute cry," and Milton's description of hell as a place with "no light, but rather darkness visible" are all examples of this process. The two words that are brought together to form a description of this kind ought to cancel each other out by the nature of their contradictions; instead, they increase the sense of each word. Thus, "sweet pain" aptly describes certain experiences of love.

Pathetic Fallacy

This is a specific kind of personification in which inanimate objects are given human emotions. John Ruskin originated the term in *Modern Painters* (1856). Ruskin uses the example of "the [ocean's] cruel crawling foam" to discuss the pathetic fallacy: The ocean is not cruel, happy to inflict pain on others, as a person may be, although it may well seem cruel to those who have suffered because of it. Ruskin obviously disapproved of such misstatement and allowed it only in verse where the poet was so moved by passion that he could not be expected to speak with greater accuracy. But in all truly great poetry, Ruskin held, the speaker is able to contain the excess emotion to express him- or herself accurately. The term is used today without this negative implication, although purists still expunge examples.

Personification

Personification is the attribution of human characteristics and/or feelings to nonhuman organisms, inanimate objects, or abstract ideas. "Death, Be Not Proud" by John Donne addresses Death as if it were a person capable of hearing as well as possessing human emotions such as pride. Tennyson's "Now sleeps the crimson petal, now the white" and Shakespeare's reference to "Time's cruel hand" are both examples of this process at work.

Romantic Irony

Romantic irony is most commonly found in German literature and shows The Creator detaching Himself from His creation to treat it playfully or objectively.

Sarcasm

Sarcasm is crude and heavy-handed verbal irony.

Simile

A *simile* is a comparison between unlike objects introduced by a connective word such as *like, as,* or *than* or a verb such as *seems.* The following are some examples of similes:

> My heart is like a singing bird. (C. Rossetti)
> I am weaker than a woman's tear. (Shakespeare)
> Seems he a dove? His feathers are but borrowed. (Shakespeare)

Socratic Irony

This form of irony is named for Socrates, who usually pretended to be ignorant when he was in fact cautious or tentative. The person who states "I do not understand; please explain this to me...." is a Socratic ironist, and his words are ironic, for he clearly *does* understand.

Symbolism

Symbolism occurs when a concrete object stands for an abstract concept. The ocean, for example, may be said to symbolize "eternity," and the phrase "river to the sea" could stand for "life flowing from afterlife." In most instances the symbol does not directly reveal what it stands for; the meaning must be discovered through a close reading of the poem and an understanding of the conventional literary and cultural symbols. For example, we realize that the "stars and stripes" stand for the American flag. We know this because we are told that it is so, for the flag in no way looks like the United States. Without cultural agreement, many of the symbols we commonly accept would be meaningless.

Synecdoche

Synecdoche substitutes a part of something for the whole or uses the whole in place of one of the parts. "Ten sails" would thus stand for ten ships. In the stanza below by the nineteenth-century American poet Emily Dickinson, "morning" and "noon," parts of the day, are used to refer to the whole day. In the same manner, "rafters of satin" refers to a coffin by describing its lining rather than the entire object:

> Safe in their Alabaster Chambers—
> Untouched by Morning
> And untouched by Noon—
> Sleep the meek members of the Resurrection—
> Rafters of satin,
> And Roof of Stone.

Synesthesia
Synesthesia takes one of the five senses and creates a picture or image of sensation as perceived by another. For example, "the golden cry of the trumpet" combines "golden," a visual perception of color, with "cry," an aspect of the sense of hearing. In the same manner, Emily Dickinson speaks of a fly's "blue, uncertain stumbling buzz."

Transferred Epithet
A *transferred epithet* is a word or phrase shifted from the noun it would usually describe to one to which it has no logical connection, as in Gray's "drowsy tinklings," where "drowsy" literally describes the sheep who wear the bells, but here is figuratively applied to the bells. In current usage, the distinction among metonymy, synecdoche, and transferred epithet is so slight that the term *metonymy* is often used to cover them all.

Understatement
Understatement is the opposite of exaggeration; it is a statement that says less than it indirectly suggests, as in Jonathan Swift's "Last week I saw a woman flayed, and you will hardly believe how much it altered her person for the worst." Auden's ironic poem "The Unknown Citizen," alluded to earlier, has a great many examples of understatement

that combine to show how numbers cannot evaluate the ultimate un-happiness of a person's life.

Verbal Irony

This form of irony involves a contrast between what is stated and what is more or less wryly suggested. The statement is somehow negated by its suggestions. Thus, Pope attacks the proud man by ironically encouraging his pride:

> Go, wiser thou! and, in thy scale of sense,
> Weigh thy opinion against Providence....
> Snatch from his hand the balance and the rod,
> Rejudge his justice, be the God of God!

What is stated ironically need not always be the direct reverse of what is suggested; irony may, for instance, state less than what is suggested, as in the following understatement: "Men have died from time to time."

Chapter 4

Types of Poems and Poetic Movements

BALLADS

The *traditional* or *popular ballad* is a story told in song form that has been passed by word of mouth from singer to singer, generation to generation. Unlike formal written verse, ballads have undergone significant change. They were common in the fifteenth century, and one, "Judas," is known to have passed down from the thirteenth century. The oral nature of a ballad is shown in the effective transitions in the narrative, for weak verse tends to get taken out and forgotten. This results in a highly effective series of pictures in words.

The tradition of the ballad runs through English and American verse. The anonymous ballads of the fifteenth century have their counterparts in the ballads of the twentieth century, in songs of social protest and stories of ordinary people. Traditional ballads were produced in America throughout the nineteenth century, commonly by sailors, loggers, and plantation workers—relatively isolated and uneducated people. In rural areas, such ballads are still flourishing today.

When professional poets write stanzas of this type, such as Auden's "I Walked Out One Evening," they are called *literary ballads*. Probably the most famous literary ballads are Coleridge's "Rime of the Ancient Mariner" and Keats's "La Belle Dame sans Merci."

The ballad stanza rhymes *abcb*. Ballads often contain *refrains*, musical repetitions of words and phrases. Some critics believe that ballads were originally two-line rhyming songs, thus explaining why there are only two rhymes in a four-line stanza. Because early ballads were non-literary, half-rhymes and slant rhymes are often used. The common stanza is a quatrain of alternating lines of iambic tetrameter and iambic trimeter. Ballads sometimes employ *incremental repetition*, the repetition of some previous line or lines, but with a slight variation to advance the narrative, as in these lines from "Sir Patrick Spens":

> The king sits in Dumferling town,
>   Drinking the blood-red wine:
> "O where will I get a good sailor,
>   To sail this ship of mine?"

Although the singers of ballads were usually common people, the subjects were often noble, and the usual theme was tragic love.

A *broadside ballad* was a poem of any sort printed on a large sheet—thus the "broadside"—and sold by street singers in the sixteenth century. Not until the eighteenth century was the word "ballad" limited to traditional narrative song.

Blank Verse

Blank verse is unrhymed iambic pentameter. It was introduced into English poetry in the middle of the sixteenth century. By the end of the century it had become the standard medium of English drama. An example, by William Shakespeare, is: "Time hath, my Lord, a wallet at his back,/Wherein he puts alms for oblivion."

Burlesque

Burlesque is not a type of verse, but any imitation of people or literary type that, by distortion, aims to amuse. Its tone is neither savage nor shrill, and it tends to ridicule faults, not serious vices. Thus it is not to be confused with *satire*, for burlesque makes fun of a minor fault with the aim of arousing amusement rather than contempt or indignation. Also, it need not make us devalue the original. For example, T.S. Eliot's "The Hollow Men" is parodied in Myra Buttle's "Sweeniad." The original reads:

> Between the conception
> And the creation
> Between the emotion
> And the response
> Falls the Shadow

The burlesque reads:

> Between the mustification
> And the deception
> Between the multiplication
> And the division
> Falls the Tower of London.

Didactic Literature

Didactic literature intends to instruct or teach. It is sometimes used in contrast to *pure poetry*, which is said to be free from instruction and moral content and intends merely to delight and entertain. The term need not be pejorative, though many use it in this manner. A good case can be made that almost all of the world's finest poetry is didactic in some way. Satire, for example, makes fun of certain modes of behavior, and Milton wrote his epic *Paradise Lost* to "justify the ways of God to men." The problem, then, is one of degree, as true didactic literature deals mainly with instruction. This does not make it any less "poetic." These lines by John Gay, explaining how to clean worms, are an example of didactic literature:

> Cherish them from filth, to give them tempting gloss,
> Cherish the sully'd reptile race with moss;
> Amid the verdant bed they twine, they toil,
> And from their bodies wipe the native soil.

Doggerel

Doggerel is verse made comic because irregular metrics are made regular by stressing normally unstressed syllables, as in Samuel Butler's lines:

> More peevish, cross, and splénetic
> Than dog distract or monkey sick;

If the subject matter is mock heroic (see previous definition), and the lines are iambic tetrameter couplets (as in the example quoted above), the poem is also referred to as *hudibrastic*, after Butler's *Hudibras*.

Dramatic Monologue

The speaker in a *dramatic monologue* is usually a fictional character or an historical figure caught in a critical moment. The speaker's words are established by the situation and are usually directed at a silent audience. These speakers usually reveal aspects of their personality of which they are unaware. To some extent, every poem is a dramatic monologue, as the individual speaker is saying something to someone, even if only to himself, but in a true dramatic monologue, the above conventions are observed. Fine examples of this mode include Robert Browning's "My Last Duchess," in which a duke who has murdered his last duchess reveals his cruelty to an emissary from his latest possible bride (see pages 94–95 for the complete poem). T. S. Eliot's "The Love Song of J. Alfred Prufrock," in which the speaker's timid self addresses his aggressively amorous self, is another example.

Elegy

An *elegy* is a poem that deals solemnly with death. In Greek and Latin verse, an elegy is a poem with alternate lines of dactylic hexameter and dactylic pentameter. Gray's "Elegy Written in a Country Churchyard" is an example in point. If an elegy is a short funeral lament, it may be called a *dirge,* which in ancient times was a funeral song. *Threnody* and *monody* are terms also used for funeral songs, although the monody is often more complex and is recited by an individual mourner. The elegy is often a *pastoral,* in which shepherds mourn the death of a fellow shepherd. They use the conventions of this type of verse, including invocation to the muses, processions of mourners, and lists of flowers. Many modern poets have used this form to great advantage, most notably Walt Whitman's elegy on Abraham Lincoln, "When Lilacs Last in the Dooryard Bloom'd."

Emblematic Poems

Emblematic poems take the shape of the subject of the poem. An emblematic poem on a swan, for example, would be in the shape of a swan. George Herbert's "Easter Wings" is an example of an emblematic poem; it is in the shape of two wings.

Epic

An *epic* is a long and serious narrative poem (a poem that tells a story) about a hero and his heroic companions. An epic is often set in a past that is pictured as greater than the present. The hero often possesses superhuman and/or divine traits. In Homer's *Iliad,* for example, the hero, Achilles, is the son of a goddess; in Milton's *Paradise Lost,* the characters are God the Father, Christ, angels, and Adam and Eve.

The action is usually rather easy to understand, such as Achilles's anger in the *Iliad* and the fall of humanity in *Paradise Lost,* but its dramatic power is increased by figurative language and allusions that often give the story cosmic importance. The style is elevated to reflect the greatness of the events, and certain traditional procedures are employed. For example, the poet usually calls to the muses for help, asking them what initiated the action (the *epic question*), and often begins the tale in the middle of the action (in *medias res*). At this point, the hero tends to be at his lowest fortunes; he only later recounts the earlier part of the tale. Gods often participate in the tale, helping the heroes. There may be a trip to Hades. The *epic simile,* also called the *Homeric simile,* is an extended comparison in which a subject is compared to something that is presented at such length or detail that the subject itself is momentarily lost in the description. For example, in *Paradise Lost,* Satan walking in Eden is compared to a vulture:

> Here walked the fiend, at large in spacious field.
> As when a vulture on Imaus bred,
> Whose snowy ridge the roving Tartar bounds,
> Dislodging from a region scarce of prey
> To gorge the flesh of lambs or yearling kids
> On hills where flocks are fed, flies toward the springs

Of Ganges or Hydaspes, Indian streams,
But in his way lights on the barren plains
Of Sericana, where Chineses drive
With sails and wind their canny wagons light;
So, on this windy sea of land, the fiend
Walked up and down alone, bent on his prey:

There are two types of epics: the *primary epic* (sometimes called the *primitive epic* or *folk epic*), a stately narrative about the noble class recited to the noble class; and the *secondary epic* (also called the *literary epic* or *artificial epic),* a stately narrative about great events designed for a literary person to read from a book. Primary epics include Homer's *Iliad* and *Odyssey* and the anonymous Old English epic *Beowulf.* Secondary epics include Virgil's *Aeneid* and Milton's *Paradise Lost.*

The poet of the primary epic speaks as the voice of the community, whereas the poet of the secondary epic may show more individuality. Homer, for example, is not introspective; Milton sometimes is. Homer's poems and *Beowulf* share discussion of aspects of an "heroic age" (virtue is identified with strength, celebrated by the poets). Because the poets in these heroic societies sang memorized poems, their chants contain a great many *stock epithets* and repeated lines. When such repetitions occur at particular positions in lines they are called *formulas,* and they serve to help the poet compose his material and remember it. An example of *formulaic poetry* is Longfellow's "The Song of Hiawatha." Modern epics include Hart Crane's *The Bridge,* William Carlos Williams's *Paterson,* and Ezra Pound's *Cantos.* The first two are examples of American epics; the last, a case for western civilization.

Epigram
Originally meaning "an inscription," the *epigram* became for the Greeks a short poem, usually solemn. But the Romans used the term to mean a short witty poem with a sting at the end. Here is an example by John Wilmont:

We have a pretty witty King,
Whose word no man relies on,
Who never said a foolish thing,
Nor did a wise one.

The term *epigram* has come to mean any cleverly expressed thought in verse or prose.

Epitaph
An *epitaph* is a burial inscription, usually serious but sometimes humorous. John Gay's own epitaph serves as an example: "Life is a jest, and all things show it;/I thought it so once, but now I know it."

Epithalamion
This is a lyric poem in honor of a bride, a bridegroom, or both. It is usually ceremonial and happy, not simply in praise of marriage but of a particular marriage. Spenser's "Epithalamion" is the greatest example in English. It begins, like its models in Greek and Roman literature, with an invocation and follows Catullus in calling on young people to attend the bride, in praising the bride, and in welcoming the night. Spenser added deep Christian feeling and realistic descriptions of landscape.

Eulogy
Frequently confused with an elegy, a *eulogy* is a poem in praise of a person or thing.

Free Verse
Free verse is composed of rhythmical lines varying in length, following no strict metrical patterns, usually unrhymed. Often, the pattern is based on repetition and follows grammatical structure. Although free verse may appear unrestrained, it does follow the rules outlined above. An example from Walt Whitman's "Song of Myself" illustrates the form of free verse:

I celebrate myself, and sing myself,
And what I assume you shall assume,
For every atom belonging to me as good as belongs to you.

Haiku

Haiku is an Oriental verse form composed of seventeen syllables in three lines. Such forms were greatly admired models for the Imagist poets, an early twentieth-century movement that attempted to shed excess words to create poems of clear, concise details.

Idyll

An *idyll* is a short, picturesque poem, usually about shepherds but sometimes in the form of an epic, also called an *epillion*. It represents an episode from the heroic past, stressing the pictoral rather than the heroic. The most famous English example is Tennyson's "Idylls of the King" with its detailed descriptions of several aspects of the Arthurian legends.

Light Verse

Light verse is considered playful poetry since it often combines light-heartedness or whimsy with mild satire. These qualities can be seen, for example, in Suckling's poem "Why So Pale and Wan, Fond Lover?" which concludes, "If of herself she will not love,/Nothing can make her;/The devil take her." The definition of light verse changed in the late nineteenth century, however, to include less polished pieces such as nursery songs with funny rhymes and distorted pronunciations.

Limerick

A *limerick* is a form of light verse, a jingling poem of three long and two short lines. The long lines (first, second, and fifth) rhyme with each other and the short lines (third and forth) rhyme with each other. The rhyming words at the end of lines can sometimes be misspelled to produce a humorous effect. The following limerick from an early sixteenth-century songbook is an example:

Once a Frenchman who'd promptly said "oui"
To some ladies who'd asked him if houi
    Cared to drink, threw a fit
    Upon finding that it
Was a tipple no stronger than toui.

Lyric

Lyrics are poems with a regular rhyme scheme and a limited length, as in the fourteen-line sonnet. Robert Burns's famous drinking song that has become the New Year's Eve staple, "Auld Lang Syne," Robert Frost's short poems, and George Herbert's religious meditations are all examples of this form. If the emotion in the poem is hate or contempt and its expression is witty, the poem is usually called a *satire*. If it is very brief, it is called an *epigram*. A *complaint* is a lyric poem expressing dissatisfaction, usually to an unresponsive lover. Chaucer's humorous "Complaint to His Purse," for example, begins, "To you, my purse, and to noon other wight,/Complayne I, for ye be my lady dere!" For a brief period in the 1800s, nature as well as love became a major subject for lyrics, and poets such as William Wordsworth expressed their thoughts of clouds and daffodils more frequently than those on love.

Macronic Verse

Macronic verse is poetry containing words resembling a foreign language or a mixture of languages. For example:

> Mademoiselle got the croix de guerre,
> For washing soldiers' underwear,
> Hinky-dinky, parlez-vous.

Mock Epic or Mock Heroic

This is also known as *high burlesque,* the reverse of travesty, for it treats minor themes in a high, lofty style. Despite its name, it does not mock the epic, but rather mocks low activities by treating them in the elevated style of the epic. The humor results from the differences between the low subject and the lofty treatment it is accorded. In the theater, a burlesque may be a play that humorously criticizes another play by making fun of aspects of it in a grotesque manner, as in John Gay's "Beggar's Opera," which makes fun of serious operas. The term is also used, especially in America, for a sort of variety show that stresses crude humor and sex.

Narrative Verse
See epic.

Nonsense Verse
See light verse.

Occasional Poems
These are poems that commemorate major occasions, such as battles, anniversaries, coronations, or any other event worthy of poetic treatment.

Ode
This poetic form was usually sung in honor of gods or heroes, but it is now usually a very long lyric poem characterized by elevated feelings. The *Pindaric ode*, named for the Greek poet Pindar (c. 522–443 B.C.), has two structurally identical stanzas, the *strophe* and *antistrophe* (Greek for "turn" and "counterturn"). These are followed by a stanza with a different structure, the *epode* (Greek for "stand"). The line length and rhyming patterns are determined by each individual poet. In the original Pindaric ode, the chorus danced a pattern while singing during the strophe, retraced the same pattern while singing during the antistrophe, and sang without dancing during the epode. The odes were characterized by great passion. Notable Pindaric odes in English are Gray's "The Progress of Poesy" and Wordsworth's "Ode: Intimations of Immortality."

Horatian odes, named after the Latin poet Horace (65–8 B.C.), are composed of matched regular stanzas of four lines that usually celebrate love, patriotism, or simple Roman morality. Notable English Horatian odes include Marvell's "Horatian Ode Upon Cromwell's Return to Ireland" and Collins's "Ode to Evening." Keats's "Ode on a Grecian Urn" is probably the best-known Horatian ode.

Although an ode is a serious poem expressing the speaker's passion, it may be passionate about almost anything. Especially during the nineteenth century, the ode tended to become less public and more personal and introspective. Shelley's "Ode to the West Wind" or Keats's "Ode to a Nightingale" are examples of this introspection. The irregular ode, such as Wordsworth's "Intimations of Immortality," has stanzas of various length, irregular rhyme schemes, and elaborate rhythms.

Sonnet

To the Elizabethans, the sonnet and the lyric were often considered one and the same, but to the modern reader, the term *sonnet* has come to mean a poem of fourteen lines (sometimes twelve or sixteen, but this is rare), written in iambic pentameter. There are two main kinds of sonnets: the *Italian* (or Petrarchan) sonnet and the *English* (or Shakespearean) sonnet.

- *The Italian sonnet*   The Italian sonnet has two divisions: the first eight lines are called the octave, rhyming *abba abba*. This section sets forth the theme of the poem, traditionally love and romance, and elaborates on it. The second section, called the sestet, rhymes *cde cde* and reflects on the theme and comes to a conclusion that ties everything together. Sidney's sonnets in English are Petrarchan, while Spenser's are linked rhymes with a variation. Milton, Wordsworth, and Keats have also written notable sonnets in the Italian form.
- *The English sonnet*   The English sonnet, in contrast, is arranged in three quatrains and a couplet, rhyming *abab cdcd efef gg*. In the English sonnet, themes and recapitulations are developed in the same way as in the Italian sonnet, but seven different rhymes are used instead of four or five.

In many sonnets, there is a marked correspondence between the rhyme scheme and the development of the main idea. Thus, the Italian sonnet gives the generalization in the octave and specific examples in the sestet. The English sonnet may give three examples, one in each quatrain, and draw a conclusion in the couplet.

A *sonnet sequence* is a group of sonnets linked by a common theme, such as love betrayed, love renewed, love itself, and so on. Some notable sonnet sequences include those by Elizabeth Barrett Browning ("Sonnets from the Portuguese"), George Meredith ("Modern Love"), W.H. Auden ("The Quest"), and Dylan Thomas ("Altarwise by Owl-light").

The *Miltonic sonnet* kept the Italian rhyme scheme, but changed the way the octet and sestet are constructed. Here, the sonnet no longer breaks at the octet but flows over and *enjambs* from line to line into the sestet. This type of sonnet appears to be more unified, beginning at one point and moving toward its inevitable conclusion. Milton also changed the theme of the typical sonnet. He moved into larger intellectual and religious concerns, a development begun by Donne.

Travesty

Also known as *low burlesque, travesty* takes a high theme and treats it in trivial terms, as in the Greek "Battle of the Frogs and Mice," which travesties Homer.

Villanelle

A *villanelle* is a poetic form that not only rhymes but also repeats lines in a predetermined manner, both as a refrain and as an important part of the poem itself. Five stanzas of three lines each are followed by a quatrain. The first and third lines of the first stanza are repeated in a prescribed alternating order as the last lines of the remaining tercets, becoming the last two lines of the final quatrain. Dylan Thomas's "Do Not Go Gentle Into That Good Night" is an example of a modern villanelle.

POETIC MOVEMENTS AND TRENDS

The following poetic movements and trends are arranged in alphabetical order, not chronological order. Keep this in mind as you read.

Aesthetic Movement

In the early nineteenth century, a devotion to beauty developed among certain literary circles in France. Beauty was thought good and desirable not because it reflected the mind of God, but because in a materialistic and chaotic world, it remained good in and of itself. This movement rejected the notion that the value of literature was related to morality—a sense of right and wrong—or some sort of usefulness. Instead, it put forth the idea that art was independent of moral or didactic (instructive) ends. This was in defiance of much of the traditional thought on the subject of art's place and purpose. The slogan was "art for art's sake" (*l'art pour l'art* in French), and many of the writers involved actively attacked the idea that art should serve any purpose in the traditional sense. In the late 1900s in England, the movement was represented by Oscar Wilde and Walter Pater. The term *fin de siècle* ("end of the century"), which earlier stood for progress, came to imply decadence—great refinement of style but a marked tendency toward abnormal or freakish content. When used as a proper noun, *Decadence* refers to the aesthetic movement.

Imagists/Imagism

At their peak between 1912 and 1914, these poets sought to use common language, to regard all the world as possible subject matter, and to present in vivid and sharp detail a concentrated visual image. "There should be no ideas but things," said poet William Carlos Williams. Imagists usually wrote free verse. The most frequently cited example of their aims is evinced in this verse by Ezra Pound, one of the leaders of the Imagist movement:

> The apparition of these faces in the crowd;
> Petals on a wet, black bough.

The title, "In a Station in the Metro," informs the reader that the poem is about a metro, a European subway, but the poem presents its meaning without directly telling the reader what conclusions to draw. To many readers, the poem suggests that the colorful faces of people in the subway are like flower petals against dark branches. The poet selects his images and arranges them; the reader must see the relationships to experience the picture the poem presents.

Imagist poets avoided the traditional accentual-syllabic rhythms and depended instead on the poem's image or picture to create a memorable effect. Poems with obvious spelled-out messages were avoided at all costs. Oriental models, most especially the seventeen-syllable three-line haiku, were much admired. Poems of all kinds contained imagery, carefully described objects of the world, but this movement went further than describing what was seen to create a theory of verse around the idea of the picture.

Metaphysical Poets

The most important Metaphysical poets include John Donne (1572–1631) and his seventeenth-century followers, Andrew Marvell, George Herbert, Abraham Cowley, Richard Crashaw, and Henry Vaughan. These poets reacted against the traditions and rules of Elizabethan love poetry to create a more witty and ironic verse. Modern critics have also concluded that the verse was more passionately intense and psychologically probing than that of the Elizabethan poets. Instead of penning smooth lines comparing a woman's beauty to something traditional such as a rose, these poets wrote colloquial and often metrically irregular lines, filled with difficult and more searching comparisons. A comparison of this nature is called a *conceit,* which came to refer to a striking parallel of two highly unlikely objects, such as the sun partly hidden by a cloud to a lover's head reclining on a pillow. Certain *Petrarchan conceits* were often used in Elizabethan poetry during this time. They included a lover as a ship tossed by a storm, shaken by his tears, frozen by the coldness of his love. The *Metaphysical conceit* is closely allied, although it may be more original than the Petrarchan conceit. New, rather than traditional, and drawn from areas not usually considered "poetic" (commerce and science, for example), metaphysical conceits usually strike the reader with an effect quite different from the Petrarchan conceit.

Pastoral

Any writing concerning itself with shepherds may be called pastoral. Often set in *Arcadia,* a mountainous area in Greece known for its simple shepherds who live uncomplicated and contented lives, a pastoral can also be called a *bucolic,* an *idyll,* or an *eclogue.* An idyll is sometimes a miniature epic, while an eclogue is usually a dialogue between two shepherds.

Rural life is usually shown to be superior to tainted city life. Christian poets sometimes added their traditions to the Greek-Roman conventions and painted the shepherd as a holy man, as Christ the Shepherd. The *georgic* is a poem dealing with rural life which, unlike the pastoral, shows a life of labor rather than a happy existence of singing and dancing throughout the day.

Chapter 5

How Poets Create a Vision

There are three basic parts to any poem: its vision, the speaker who expresses that vision, and the language the poet uses to create voice and vision. This section will examine the ways in which language creates that vision.

When we use the term "vision" in relationship to verse, we are saying that the poet's vision is shared by the audience. By the end of a successful poem, then, we should have something that we recognize, perhaps even a reflection of our inner selves as we have not before experienced it.

There are two ways in which a poet can create this successful vision. The first is to express his or her views so clearly that we feel that we are seeing what the poet wishes us to see with a new closeness and clarity. The second way involves using figures of speech or unexpected comparisons or juxtapositions of words to force us to make comparisons we have never before imagined. A look at two poems that use these different methods will show how language operates in each:

The Dalliance of the Eagles

Skirting the river road, (my forenoon walk, my rest,)
Skyward in air a sudden muffled sound, the dalliance of the eagles,
The rushing amorous contact high in space together,
The clinching interlocking claws, a living, fierce, gyrating wheel,
Four beating wings, two beaks, a swirling mass tight grappling,
In tumbling turning clustering loops, straight downward falling,
Till o'er the river pois'd, the twain yet one, a moment's lull,

A motionless still balance in the air, then parting, talons loosing,
Upward again on slow-firm pinions slanting, their separate
      diverse flight,
She hers, he his, pursuing.

—*Walt Whitman*

The Eagle: A Fragment

He clasps the crag with crooked hands;
Close to the sun in lonely lands,
Ringed with the azure world, he stands.

The wrinkled sea beneath him crawls:
He watches from his mountain walls,
And like a thunderbolt he falls.

—*Alfred, Lord Tennyson*

It is easy to see that these poems are very different. Tennyson's work, depicting a lone eagle who remains still throughout most of the poem, creates a feeling of space and solitude; Whitman's poem, dealing with two eagles, seems to have captured a constant rush of movement. The difference in feeling is created in part by the sounds of the words the poets have selected. Tennyson's words, lines, and sentences are all short, and the stops at the end of each line are sharply marked. Whitman, in contrast, uses longer lines, with less sharp breaks between them, and his sentences are complex and involved. This technique keeps the reader's mind in almost constant motion—like that of the eagles' flight. Yet the basic difference in the presentation of these two poems lies not in the motion of the eagles, but rather in the imagery used to describe them.

Imagery: Whitman

A close examination of the poems reveals this difference in imagery. Whitman uses a great many adjectives, especially participles (adjectives formed from verbs). These include, for example, *clinching, interlocking, living, beating,* and *grappling.* These participles convey a sense of motion and action and contribute much to the force of the poem's description. The poet is an observer here. Taking a walk, he has been startled first by the "sudden muffled sound" and then by the sight of the eagles. He describes these two sensations as carefully and as fully as he can: "The clinching interlocking claws, a living, fierce, gyrating wheel,/ Four beating wings, two beaks, a swirling mass tight grappling."

Imagery: Tennyson

Tennyson's verse is also descriptive, but it varies greatly from Whitman's in the types of words he chooses to describe the eagle. Where Whitman uses words that could easily be applied to eagles, Tennyson uses words that are not usually associated with birds. His eagle is described in terms that compare it to other things: an old man, grown crooked with age; an explorer in "lonely lands"; a thunderbolt. By calling our attention to the comparison between the eagle and other objects, Tennyson draws upon our feelings for these other objects (respect or awe, for example) and uses these emotions to influence our feelings about the eagle itself. Thus, instead of saying, as Whitman does, that the eagle has "clinching…claws," Tennyson gives his eagle "crooked hands." He "stands"—a human rather than a birdlike thing to do—and "watches" as both men and birds do. The landscape is also humanized. The lands are described as "lonely," the sea is pictured as "wrinkled" and it "crawls." There are examples of hyperbole (exaggeration) as well. The eagle is said to have a perch "close to the sun," which of course is impossible. In the same way, the sky against which he is pictured is an entire "azure world," and the eagle falls like a "thunderbolt." High and remote, yet in these qualities very human, Tennyson's eagle presents a stunning image of a creature in isolation.

Conclusion

By linking things that we would not ourselves associate, the poets create new images and call forth new emotions that make the reader look at things in a different light. Abstract ideas become specific through the use of precise visual images and specific words. The reader derives very different feelings from Whitman's waterfall of precisely denotative adjectives and Tennyson's careful balance of connotations of space, people, and isolation. A closer look at other forms of comparisons can show us how imagery works in different settings. Comparative figures of speech include explicit comparisons, similes and metaphors, implicit comparisons, implied metaphors, and personification.

SIMILES, METAPHORS, AND PERSONIFICATION

One Method for Reading Poetry

One way to read a poem is to scan it once, then go back and note all the figures of speech. Identify each one and decide what elements make up the comparison—what is being compared to what. Make some notes about why the poet would want readers to think about these specific comparisons. Then, read the poem through once again. Look at the figures of speech that you have noted and see how each relates to the meaning of the poem. Decide what the speaker's feelings are toward the subject and how many subjects of comparison there are. Here are some questions you may wish to ask yourself:

- Is each subject compared to one thing, or is one subject compared to many?
- Is the comparison developed at length? If so, to what purpose?
- What is the point that the poet is making through the comparison?
- If the subject is related to several things, how do the different images fit together?
- Are they unrelated, leaving it to the reader to create a pattern of meaning?
- Or does the poet suggest some sort of relationship or contrast between them?
- How does the pattern thus created form your sense of the poet's vision?

Finally, read the poem through once again to see that the conclusions you have reached make sense. This may look like a very complex and time-consuming process, but it is an effective way for studying verse. It is especially handy for exams when you are expected to be fully aware of the poet's techniques and must be able to discuss how and why the poet selected specific images and figures of speech. Of course, poetry may be read in many other ways, but this method will help you gain a clear understanding of the poem's form and content.

Similes

Similes are comparisons using the words "like" or "as" or similar words of comparison. Usually the objects under comparison resemble each other in only one or two ways, differing in all other ways. For example, an eagle and a thunderbolt are really not very much alike, but the fact that they both can travel from the sky to the ground allows Tennyson to use this comparison to say that the eagle falls "like a thunderbolt." The strength of the simile lies in the difference between the eagle and the thunderbolt. The fact that the thunderbolt is much more powerful and dangerous than the eagle gives a sense of speed, power, and danger to the bird's fall.

Langston Hughes constructed an entire poem, "Harlem," on the basis of similes. He compared a dream that has been put off to various physical items that have in some manner changed their appearance. He calls forth the image of a raisin, a dried grape, and a cut that has become infected. All the similes he uses in some way appeal to our senses and tell us that deferring our dreams will cause horrible things to happen. No matter how the change occurs, lives will not remain untouched by the disappointment of deferred dreams. While the structure and language of the poem are simple, at least on the surface, the similes lend extraordinary power to the poem's theme (main idea).

Metaphors

Like similes, *metaphors* are comparisons of two unlike objects. In this instance, though, the joining of the two objects is more concrete, for there is no intervening word such as "like" or "as." Instead, the metaphor simply states that A *is* B; one element of the comparison becomes the other. Some metaphors go one step further and omit the word "is." These metaphors talk about A as though it were B, and in some cases may not even use the name for B at all, forcing the reader to guess what B is by the language used. In this instance, the metaphor is called an *implied metaphor.*

The following poem by John Keats makes use of metaphors:

On First Looking into Chapman's Homer

Much have I travell'd in the realms of gold,
 And many goodly states and kingdoms seen;
 Round many western islands have I been
Which bards in fealty to Apollo hold.
5 Oft of one wide expanse had I been told
  That deep-browed Homer ruled as his demesne;
  Yet did I never breathe its pure serene
Till I heard Chapman speak out loud and bold:
Then felt I like some watcher of the skies
10 When a new planet swims into his ken;
Or like stout Cortez when with eagle eyes
  He star'd at the Pacific—and all his men
Look'd at each other with a wild surmise—
  Silent, upon a peak in Darien.

—John Keats

The vocabulary in the first eight lines of this poem is drawn mainly from the Middle Ages and its system of feudalism. The word "realms" is used for *kingdoms,* "bards" for *poets,* and "fealty" for the system under which a nobleman owed his allegiance to a king or other nobleman with more extensive power. "Demesne" is the word for the nobleman's *domain,* and "ken" often means *knowledge.* "Serene" means *air,* and "oft" means *often.* Apollo, in contrast, is drawn from classical mythology and stands for the god of poets. Homer is an ancient Greek poet and Chapman a sixteenth-century English poet who was noted for his translation of Homer's *Iliad* into English. What we must ask ourselves, then, is why the poet would use the language of the Middle Ages and the metaphor of traveling to talk about his joy in reading poetry and the delight he experienced when his discovery of Chapman's translations made him feel that he was reading Homer for the first time. Perhaps he selected the Middle Ages metaphor to show the timelessness of true poetry, how it transcends the boundaries of time to speak for all people. Below are some further questions to consider:

Questions to Consider:
1. When Keats finds Chapman's translations, two new similes come to him that support the metaphor of the traveler. What is the first, found in lines 9–10? How does the new identity of the poet resemble his earlier pose as a traveler? How is it different? What sorts of feelings go with each identity?
2. The second simile appears in lines 11–14. Who does the poet feel like now? How do his new feelings form a climax to the poem?

Answers:
1. In lines 9–10, the poet compares his feelings to those of an astronomer discovering a new planet.
2. In lines 11–14, he compares his feelings to those of an explorer (Cortez) discovering a new ocean (the Pacific). From these two similes we can sense the poet's great excitement and wonder.

NB: It will make no difference to your enjoyment of the poem, but Balboa, not Cortez, was the first European to see the Pacific Ocean.

Personification
Personification is a type of implied metaphor, in this instance, speaking about something nonliving as though it were living. Or, in the case of Tennyson's eagle, the attribution of human characteristics ("crooked hands") to something nonhuman (the bird).

Try Your Hand!
Put it all together by analyzing these poems. Look for similes, metaphors, personification. See what meaning you can discover.

from A Pindaric Ode

It is not growing like a tree
In bulk, doth make man better be;
Or, standing long an oak, three hundred year,
To fall a log at last, dry, bald, and sear:
    A lily of a day
    Is fairer far, in May,
    Although it fall and die that night;
    It was the plant and flower of light.
In small proportions we just beauties see,
And in short measures life may perfect be.

—Ben Jonson

Composed Upon Westminster Bridge,
September 3, 1802

Earth has not any thing to show more fair:
Dull would he be of soul who could pass by
A sight so touching in its majesty:
This City now doth, like a garment, wear
The beauty of the morning; silent, bare,
Ships, towers, domes, theatres, and temples lie
Open unto the fields, and to the sky;
All bright and glittering in the smokeless air.
Never did sun more beautifully steep
In his first splendor, valley, rock, or hill;
Ne'er saw I, never felt, a calm so deep!
The river glideth at his own sweet will:
Dear God! the very houses seem asleep;
And all that mighty heart is lying still!

—William Wordsworth

Discussion

Most metaphors have a certain timelessness to them, a quality that en-
dures through the ages. For example, Wordsworth's picture of London
asleep holds the same freshness for us today as it held during his era.

SYMBOL AND ALLEGORY

Introduction
Similes and metaphors tend to make their points quickly, for they occupy little more than a line or two. They can be linked to others of their kind to make further points, or they may stand alone, secure in their power. Symbol and allegory, in contrast, tend to dominate the poems in which they are used. Further, they tend to stand alone and are not piled upon one another as similes and metaphors often are. One symbol or allegorical device is usually all that a poem can maintain.

Similes and metaphors are used to make us take a closer look at a subject or to look at a subject in a new light. Symbols and allegory, in contrast, force us to look beyond the literal meaning of the poem's statement or action. The following poem provides an example:

The Tyger

Tyger! Tyger! burning bright
In the forests of the night,
What immortal hand or eye
Could frame thy fearful symmetry?

In what distant deeps or skies
Burnt the fire of thine eyes?
On what wings dare he aspire?
What the hand dare seize the fire?

And what shoulder, & what art,
Could twist the sinews of thy heart?
And when thy heart began to beat,
What dread hand? & what dread feet?

What the hammer? what the chain?
In what furnace was thy brain?
What the anvil? what dread grasp
Dare its deadly terrors clasp?

When the stars threw down their spears,
And water'd heaven with their tears,
Did he smile his work to see?
Did he who made the Lamb make thee?

Tyger! Tyger! burning bright
In the forests of the night,
What immortal hand or eye
Dare frame thy fearful symmetry?

—*William Blake*

Discussion
In this poem, Blake wishes to focus our attention not on the topic of tigers but on the awesome qualities suggested by the tiger's beauty and godlike powers involved in its creation. This poem may lead the reader to the question of the existence of evil as symbolized by the tiger's murderous nature. How far the symbol or allegory is carried is frequently left in the reader's hands.

Allegory
Allegory always tells of an action. The events of the action should make literal sense, but they carry much more meaning in a nonliteral interpretation. Usually that second interpretation will have a spiritual or psychological level of meaning, for allegories tend to use physical actions to describe the workings of the mind. Thus, allegory presents correspondence between some physical action (usually some sort of encounter) and a second action (usually psychological or physical), with each step of the literal tale matching the allegorical one. Symbolism, too, may involve the use of a tale, but it may also set forth a description of some unchanging being or object. And it's far more likely to suggest several different interpretations than to insist on a single one. The following poem, for instance, presents a symbolic tale of a king's fall from power:

Ozymandias

I met a traveller from an antique land,
Who said —"Two vast and trunkless legs of stone
Stand in the desert...Near them, on the sand,
Half sunk a shattered visage lies, whose frown,
And wrinkled lip, and sneer of cold command,
Tell that its sculptor well those passions read
Which yet survive, stamped on these lifeless things,
The hand that mocked them, and the heart that fed;
And on the pedestal, these words appear:
My name is Ozymandias, King of Kings,
Look on my Works, ye Mighty, and despair!
Nothing beside remains. Round the decay
Of that colossal Wreck, boundless and bare
The lone and level sands stretch far away."

—*Percy Bysshe Shelley*

Discussion

The whole tale of the king's loss of power is symbolic, but within the tale, the most striking symbol is the broken statue with its boastful inscription. For many readers, the vision of the statue comes to mind when anyone says "Ozymandias." The full story of the king tends to come as an afterthought.

And what of the symbolism here? Does the king's loss of power symbolize the fall of the proud, which would lend a moral interpretation to the poem? Or is it rather the fall of tyranny, which would throw a political cast on the poem's theme? Or is it simply the inescapable destruction of human lives and civilization by the unceasing motion of time?

All three levels of meaning can be read into the poem's symbol, and this contributes to the lasting power of the work. Without doubt, the tyrant with his "sneer of cold command" seems unsavory enough for the reader to welcome his overthrow. But the sculptor, with the "hand that mocked," is dead too, and even the work that was to endure is half destroyed. The picture this sonnet paints is simple enough on the surface; the interpretation of the symbol gives it additional strength.

Look for the symbolism in the following poem:

The Lamb

Little Lamb, who made thee?
Dost thou know who made thee?
Gave thee life & bid thee feed,
By the stream & o'er the mead;
Gave thee clothing of delight,
Softest clothing woolly bright;
Gave thee such a tender voice,
Making all the vales rejoice!
Little Lamb who made thee?
Dost thou know who made thee?

Little Lamb I'll tell thee,
Little Lamb I'll tell thee!
He is callèd by thy name,
For he calls himself a Lamb:
He is meek & he is mild,
He became a little child;
I a child & thou a lamb,
We are callèd by his name.
Little Lamb God bless thee.
Little Lamb God bless thee.

—*William Blake*

Discussion

Here, Blake is relying on the traditional association of Christ with the lamb, and thus the meaning is less difficult to discern than in other poems where the author may invent a private symbol and an interpretation as well.

CONCEITS AND ALLUSIONS

Because they are so easy to recognize and usually easy to understand, similes and metaphors are the first kind of figurative language we notice when we are reading verse. Symbols and allegories need a much closer reading but are rewarding because they offer richness and a deep resonance. *Conceits* and *allusions* may be brief or run the entire length of the poem, but in either case, they tend to be the most difficult figures of speech to discern, often requiring some outside knowledge to make their meaning clear.

Conceits

A *conceit* is a comparison between two unlike objects; some have even called it an "outrageous metaphor." Conceits are usually developed at length, comparing and contrasting two different aspects of the two objects to make their meaning clear. In love verse, conceits often derive from the Renaissance tradition that paints the woman as the walled village and the man as the conquering hero; he attacks and she defends or surrenders. Or she might be the warrior, harming him with sharp looks and sharp words. She could be depicted as a goddess of love—the list goes on and on. Some poets take these poetic conventions very seriously; others use them in fun, capitalizing on the shock that comes from turning an expected comparison upside down.

The Metaphysical Conceits of the Seventeenth Century

The unexpected was a crucial part of the poetic conceit for the Metaphysical poets of the seventeenth century. They used conceits in religious verse as well as love verse and succeeded in forging poetry of great complexity. Any of the sciences—physics, astronomy, navigation—could yield a conceit that charted the soul's progress in relation to the physical universe. Such metaphysical conceits can be very difficult to understand, but they can be very rewarding for the depth of vision they offer.

The following poem provides examples of the use of metaphysical conceits. Note that there are two main groups of imagery in this poem. The first concerns maps and voyages; the second is the image of Christ as a second Adam. Also note that the two images are interwoven by the idea of the soul's journey to salvation as an annihilation of time and space and by the physical image of the sick man, flat on his back in bed and suffering with fever.

Hymn to God My God, in My Sickness

Since I am coming to that holy room
    Where, with thy choir of saints for evermore,
I shall be made thy music; as I come
      I tune the instrument here at the door,
      And what I must do then, think now before.

Whilst my physicians by their love are grown
    Cosmographers, and I their map, who lie
Flat on this bed, that by them may be shown
      That this is my southwest discovery
      Per fretum febris, by these straits to die,

I joy, that in these straits, I see my West;
    For, though their currents yield return to none,
What shall my West hurt me? As West and East
      In all flat maps (and I am one) are one,
      So death doth touch the resurrection.

Is the Pacific Sea my home? Or are
    The Eastern riches? Is Jerusalem?
Anyan, and Magellan, and Gibraltar,
      All straits, and none but straits, are ways to them,
      Whether where Japhet dwelt, or Cham, or Shem.

We think that Paradise and Calvary,
    Christ's Cross, and Adam's tree, stood in one place;
Look, Lord, and find both Adams met in me;
      As the first Adam's sweat surrounds my face,
      May the last Adam's blood my soul embrace.

So, in his purple wrapped, receive me, Lord;
> By these his thorns give me his other crown;
And, as to others' souls I preached thy word,
> Be this my text, my sermon to mine own:
Therefore that he may raise the Lord throws down.

—John Donne

Discussion

Conceits demand that we bring some outside knowledge to our understanding of the poem under study. For example, we must be able to grasp the distortions of space involved in making a flat map represent a round world if we are to fully grasp Donne's hymn. In the same way, an allusion demands that we bring outside knowledge to our reading. An *allusion* is a reference to a previous work of literature or to some well-known poem or event. If we do not understand the reference, we may misunderstand the poem.

Notice how the speakers in the three poems that follow use conceits or allusions to praise the women they love and to expound on the benefits of love. Begin by looking carefully at the imagery in each poem. Then note the apostrophes (direct address) and the differing tones used in each poem.

From Amoretti—Sonnet 15

Ye tradefull Merchants, that with weary toyle,
Do seeke most precious things to make your gain,
And both the Indias of their treasure spoile,
What needeth you to seeke so farre in vaine?
5 For loe, my love doth in her selfe containe,
All this world's riches that may farre be found:
If saphyres, loe her eies be saphyres plaine;
If rubies, loe her lips be rubies sound;
If pearles hir teeth be pearles both pure and round;
10 If yvorie, her forehead yvory weene;
If gold, her locks are finest gold on ground;
If silver, her faire hands are silver sheene:

But that which fairest is but few behold:—
Her mind, adorn'd with vertues manifold.

—Edmund Spenser

Questions to Consider:
1. Toward whom is the poet addressing his remarks? Hint: Focus on the first four lines.
2. Why should the poet select this particular audience?
3. What do the phrases "weary toyle" and "in vaine" suggest about the poet's audience or their activities?
4. How are the metaphors in lines 7–12 connected?
5. How does the conclusion continue the theme of treasure? How does it change the theme?
6. What new questions does the conclusion raise about the merchants' quest for precious things?

Answers:
1. The poet is addressing merchants.
2. He might have selected the merchants because they traveled far and wide to seek riches, in contrast to the poet's feeling that all the riches of the world are right at home, in the person of his loved one.
3. The words suggest that the travels are useless, for real treasure is found in love, not commodities.
4. The poet describes the beauty of his love in terms of the most precious substances on earth: gems, gold, silver, and ivory.
5. The conclusion fits with the theme of treasure in that the mind of the poet's loved one is also "adorn'd" with riches. It changes the theme since the mind cannot really be seen, and her virtues, the most valuable of her treasures, cannot be gathered like so many jewels.
6. According to the poet, the merchants' quest is absurd, for all we should seek are the virtues hidden in a fine mind, not the outward show of precious metals and stones.

Here's another poem to consider. As with the previous sonnet, this one also starts with questions relating to physical qualities and concludes with questions relating to intangible elements. Read the poem through several times and then answer the questions that follow.

Sonnet 18

Shall I compare thee to a summer's day?
Thou art more lovely and more temperate:
Rough winds do shake the darling buds of May,
And summer's lease hath all too short a date:
5   Sometime too hot the eye of heaven shines
And often is his gold complexion dimmed;
And every fair from fair sometimes declines,
By chance or nature's changing course untrimmed;
But thy eternal summer shall not fade,
10 Nor lose possession of that fair thou ow'st;
Nor shall death brag thou wander'st in his shade,
When in eternal lines to time thou grow'st:
So long as men can breathe, or eyes can see,
So long lives this, and this gives life to thee.

—*William Shakespeare*

Questions to Consider:

1. By means of what comparisons does Shakespeare achieve this movement from tangible to intangible?
2. Trace the poet's logic to show how he arrived at the movement in question 1.
3. Compare and contrast this poem to *Sonnet 15* by Spenser. How are they the same? How are they different?

Answers:

1. Shakespeare compares a woman's beauty to the beauty of a summer's day to conclude that art—in the form of this sonnet—insures her immortality. The final line, "So long lives this [the sonnet], and this gives life to thee," sums up the movement from tangible to intangible.
2. See lines 1–12 for the development of the theme. The final couplet presents the conclusion and makes the poet's point. Note especially

the phrases "summer's day" (line 1), "the eye of heaven" (line 5), and "eternal summer" (line 9). These phrases signal the beginning of the three phases of the author's argument, with the final two lines marking the conclusion. Also, be aware that "fair" had three meanings in Shakespeare's day: a noun meaning "a lovely thing," an adjective meaning "lovely," and a noun meaning "beauty."

3. Both poems are the same in that they praise a loved one for her appearance. They are different in that Shakespeare's sonnet makes the specific point that this particular poem will immortalize the subject.

Try the same technique with the following poem. Once again, read the poem through several times; then answer the question that follows.

The Sun Rising

Busy old fool, unruly sun,
    Why dost thou thus
Through windows and through curtains call on us?
Must to thy motions lovers' seasons run?
    Saucy, pedantic wretch, go chide
    Late schoolboys and sour prentices,
Go tell court huntsmen that the King will ride,
Call country ants to harvest offices;
Love, all alike, no season knows nor clime,
Nor hours, days, months, which are the rags of time.

Thy beams, so reverend and strong
    Why shouldst thou think?
I could eclipse and cloud them with a wink,
But that I would not lose her sight so long;
    If her eyes have not blinded thine,
    Look, and tomorrow late, tell me,
Whether both th' Indias of spice and mine
Be where thou leftst them, or lie here with me.
Ask for those kings whom thou saw'st yesterday,
And thou shalt hear, All here in one bed lay.

> She is all states, and all princes, I,
>   Nothing else is.
> Princes do but play us; compared to this,
> All honor's mimic, all wealth alchemy.
>   Thou, sun, art half as happy as we,
>   In that the world's contracted thus;
>   Thine age asks ease, and since thy duties be
>   To warm the world, that's done in warming us.
>   Shine here to us, and thou art everywhere;
>   This bed thy center is, these walls thy sphere.

—*John Donne*

Question to Consider:

Here again earthly riches are equated with the beauty of a woman and then devalued by it, as time gives way to timelessness. How does Donne's treatment of these conceits differ from those of Shakespeare and Spenser? How is it the same?

Answer:

Donne's treatment is different from that of Shakespeare in that he is not saying that this poem will afford the woman immortality. Also, Shakespeare does not place the woman in the center of the universe, as does Donne in this line: "This bed thy center is, these walls thy sphere." Of the three, you could make a case for Spenser's poem being the least sophisticated, because he simply praises the woman for her beauty and virtues, while the other two poems make further arguments. Donne's poem is far more earthy than either Shakespeare's or Spenser's, as it makes specific references to the woman's love.

IMAGERY

Introduction

We have isolated the different figures of speech to discuss each one individually and to provide examples, but in actual practice, the various poetic devices are almost always found in combination with one another. Just as form and meaning serve to reinforce each other, so a poem's figures of speech work together to echo the poem's pattern of meaning and imagery. When you first begin to read a poem, you may focus on one striking aspect of it, but once you have studied the poem in depth, its entire pattern should come together and the various figures of speech will combine to help you understand the poem's meaning.

Definition

An *image* is a word or phrase that appeals to the senses—sight, smell, taste, touch, or sound—in such a way as to suggest objects or their characteristics. Images serve to create pictures in the reader's mind and aid in conveying the poem's theme.

Renaissance poems tended to begin with a position and then build on it, showing little movement within the verse. Metaphysical poems showed more movement; they often followed a speaker's mind through the ramifications of an idea or situation. Modern poetry may create scenes, moods, and speakers with even greater movement and further use of sound and imagery. The nineteenth-century American poet Walt Whitman, for example, relied on a pattern of imagery rather than on more conventional rhymes and meters to structure his verse. Whitman's "There Was a Child Went Forth" is one example. As you read the poem, focus on the imagery. Then answer the questions that follow.

There Was a Child Went Forth

There was a child went forth every day,
And the first object he look'd upon, that object he became,
And that object became part of him for the day or a certain part
    of the day,
Or for many years or stretching cycles of years.

5   The early lilacs became part of this child,
And grass and white and red morning-glories, and white and
    red clover, and the song of the phoebe-bird,
And the Third-month lambs and the sow's pink-faint litter, and
    the mare's foal and the cow's calf,

And the noisy brood of the barnyard or by the mire of the
    pond-side,
And the fish suspending themselves so curiously below there,
    and the beautiful curious liquid,
10 And the water-plants with their graceful flat heads, all became
    part of him.

The field-sprouts of Fourth-month and Fifth-month became
    part of him,
Winter-grain sprouts and those of the light-yellow corn, and the
    esculent roots of the garden,
And the apple-trees cover'd with blossoms and the fruit
    afterwards, and woodberries, and the commonest weeds by
    the road,
And the old drunkard staggering home from the outhouse of
    the tavern whence he had lately risen,
15 And the schoolmistress that pass'd on her way to the school,
And the friendly boys that pass'd, and the quarrelsome boys,
And the tidy and fresh-cheek'd girls, and the barefoot negro boy
    and girl,
And all the changes of city and country wherever he went.

His own parents, he that had father'd him and she that had
    conceiv'd him in her womb and birth'd him,
20 They gave this child more of themselves than that,
They gave him afterward every day, they became part of him.

The mother at home quietly placing the dishes on the supper-
    table,
The mother with mild words, clean her cap and gown, a
    wholesome odor falling off her person and clothes as she
    walks by,
The father, strong, self-sufficient, manly, mean, anger'd, unjust,
25 The blow, the quick loud word, the tight bargain, the crafty
    lure,
The family usages, the language, the company, the furniture,
    the yearning and swelling heart,

Affection that will not be gainsay'd, the sense of what is real, the
    thought if after all it should prove unreal,
The doubts of day-time and the doubts of night-time, the
    curious whether and how,
Whether that which appears so is so, or is it all flashes and
    specks?
30 Men and women crowding fast in the streets, if they are not
    flashes and specks what are they?
The streets themselves and the façades of houses, and goods in
    the windows,
Vehicles, teams, the heavy-plank'd wharves, the huge crossing at
    the ferries,
The village on the highland seen from afar at sunset, the river
    between,
Shadows, aureola and mist, the light falling on roofs and gables
    of white or brown two miles off,
35 The schooner near by sleepily dropping down the tide, the little
    boat slack-tow'd astern,
The hurrying, tumbling waves, quick-broken crests, slapping,
The strata of color'd clouds, the long bar of maroon-tint away
    solitary by itself, the spread of purity it lies motionless in,
The horizon's edge, the flying sea-crow, the fragrance of salt
    marsh and shore mud,
These became part of that child who went forth every day, and
    who now goes, and will always go forth every day.

—Walt Whitman

Questions to Consider:
1. Describe the image in each of the following groups of lines: 1–13, 14–17, 19–26, 30–34, 35–38.
2. Do these images form a pattern? If so, what is it?
3. How does the imagery serve to unify and connect the poem?
4. Discuss the meaning of lines 19–21. How did the child's parents become "part of him"?
5. What is the poet describing through the use of images in line 37?
6. How long is the time span in the poem?

Answers:

1. Lines 1–13: Spring morning in the country, the beginning of both plant and animal life;

   Lines 14–17: Fall and re-entry into the town and the world of people;

   Lines 19–26: Home and the child's parents;

   Lines 30–34: The movement of the city;

   Lines 35–38: The shore and nightfall.

2. There are several patterns evident here: There is movement from childhood to adulthood, from home to shore, from morning to evening, from country to city, from self outward to others, from season to season (spring-summer-fall), from acceptance to doubt, and finally back to reaffirmation of life and the goodness of the universe.

3. All the images are connected to the child. He embraces the country and the city, land and water, spring and fall, and so on. He is the link that connects all the various pictures the poet creates.

4. The child is more than the result of love between his parents. He is a creation whose development depends on the continued care of his parents. They present him with lessons on how to live, lessons that the child blends into his own self-image.

5. Sunset over the water is the image described here.

6. The poem takes place over one day, from sunrise to sunset.

Now analyze the images in the following poem by English poet Robert Browning.

Meeting at Night

1

The gray sea and the long black land;
And the yellow half-moon large and low;
And the startled little waves that leap
In fiery ringlets from their sleep,
As I gain the cove with pushing prow,
And quench its speed i' the slushy sand.

2

Then a mile of warm sea-scented beach;
Three fields to cross till a farm appears;
A tap at the pane, the quick sharp scratch
And blue spurt of a lighted match,
And a voice less loud, through its joys and fears,
Than the two hearts beating each to each!

—*Robert Browning*

Discussion

This is a poem about love, but despite the number of things we can infer about love—it is a sweet and exciting time when everything seems beautiful and the most minor things seem significant—nothing is told to us directly. As a matter of fact, the author does not even use the word "love" in the poem. He is conveying an experience to the audience. He accomplishes this by presenting a situation—a man going to meet his love—and describing the situation so clearly in terms of sensory impressions that the reader is able to share the poet's experience.

Every line in the poem centers about an image: the gray sea, the long black land, the yellow half-moon, the blue spurt of the lighted match. These images allow the reader to experience the poet's world and to become a part of it. The warm sea smell of the beach appeals to both our sense of smell and touch while the lovers' quiet speech sparks our sense of hearing. By engaging the reader's senses, the poet is able to attract the reader's attention and convey his feelings on the subject of love.

Read the following two poems by Edgar Allan Poe. Then answer the questions that follow.

Annabel Lee

It was many and many a year ago,
    In a kingdom by the sea
That a maiden there lived whom you may know.
    By the name of ANNABEL LEE;
5 And this maiden she lived with no other thought
    Than to love and be loved by me.

I was a child and *she* was a child,
    In this kingdom by the sea;
But we loved with a love that was more than love—
10   I and my ANNABEL LEE;
With a love that the wingèd seraphs of heaven
    Coveted her and me.

And this was the reason that, long ago,
    In this kingdom by the sea,
15 A wind blew out of a cloud, chilling
    My beautiful ANNABEL LEE;
So that her highborn kinsmen came
    And bore her away from me,
To shut her up in a sepulcher
20   In this kingdom by the sea.

The angels, not half so happy in heaven,
    Went envying her and me—
Yes!—that was the reason (as all men know,
    In this kingdom by the sea)
25 That the wind came out of the cloud by night,
    Chilling and killing my ANNABEL LEE.

But our love it was stronger by far than the love
    Of those who were older than we—
    Of many far wiser than we—
30 And neither the angels in heaven above,
    Nor the demons down under the sea,
Can ever dissever my soul from the soul
    Of the beautiful ANNABEL LEE:

For the moon never beams, without bringing me dreams
35   Of the beautiful ANNABEL LEE;
And the stars never rise, but I feel the bright eyes
    Of the beautiful ANNABEL LEE;
And so, all the night-tide, I lie down by the side
Of my darling,—my darling—my life and my bride,
40   In the sepulcher there by the sea.
    In her tomb by the sounding sea.

To Helen

Helen, thy beauty is to me
    Like those Nicéan barks of yore,
That gently, o'er a perfumed sea,
    The weary, wayworn wanderer bore
5   To his own native shore.

On desperate seas long wont to roam,
    Thy hyacinth hair, thy classic face,
Thy Naiad airs, have brought me home
    To the Glory that was Greece,
10 And the grandeur that was Rome.

Lo! in yon brilliant window-niche
    How statue-like I see thee stand,
    The agate lamp within thy hand!
Ah, Psyche, from the regions which
15   Are Holy Land!

Questions to Consider:

1. Characterize the descriptions of women in these two poems. How are they alike?

2. The meaning of "To Helen" depends on the classical imagery in which it is expressed. What parallel does Poe draw between Helen and the "Nicean barks" in the first stanza?

3. How does the simile in the previous question serve to describe the poet himself?

4. Find the metaphors in the second and third stanzas of "To Helen." Then, show how they reinforce Poe's theme. What is the theme of this poem?

5. In either poem, find examples of the following types of figurative language:
   - alliteration
   - assonance
   - repetition

6. Find examples of rhyme in both poems. Look especially for end rhyme.

Answers:

1. While it appears that women are at the center of both poems, these women seem less than real. What we have here are idealized portraits, removed and abstract. The woman in each poem is untouchable—Annabel Lee because she is firmly in the grave, Helen because she is set so high on a pedestal of classical perfection that it seems impossible to see in her any human qualities. In fact, "To Helen" has a line that sums this up: "How statue-like I see thee stand."

2. Poe compares Helen's beauty to a ship, for it can carry him to the heights of happiness experienced by a weary traveler brought home at last. The meaning of this poem has been much discussed and debated. It may be that the poet was drawing from the people of what is now Nice, France, who were a great sea power in the latter part of the Middle Ages. The phrase "perfumed sea" calls forth the image of Nicea (now called Iznik), located just southeast of the Bosporus. This city was important because it was located on the early trade routes to the Orient, but it was not on the sea. The Phoenicians—"lovers of the sea"—are another reference to classical imagery. They were the ones to whom Odysseus recounted his adventures and who sent him home in their enchanted bark (ship).

3. This simile shows the poet, exhausted by his travels on the sea of life, finding succor in thoughts of Helen's ideal beauty, which he seems to link to the happy days of his youth.

4. "Hyacinth hair" serves to call forth the images of beauty and makes a classical reference to Hyacinthus. "Naiad airs" may refer to the Ulysses story and also reinforces the impression of beauty. "Psyche" in the third stanza is also a classical reference. Psyche was separated from her lover, Cupid, when she ignored his instructions and took a lamp to look for him. She searched for Cupid for years, and finally she was reunited with him. The theme of this poem revolves around the contemplation of Helen's beauty. By thinking of Helen, the

ideally remembered figure from his childhood, the poet is able to recapture the classic beauty of the state of mind he enjoyed during his youth. He implies that this state of mind must have been common when the world itself was "young"—in the classical age.

5. *Alliteration,* the repetition of the initial sound of two or more closely related words, is found, for example, in the last stanza of *Annabel Lee.* Line 40 has "sepulcher," and "sea" and line 41, "sounding" and "sea."

   Assonance, the sound of the vowel repeated in two or more accented syllables, can also be found in the last stanza of *Annabel Lee.* The long *e* sounds of the internally rhymed words *beams* and *dreams* (line 34) also appear in the *me* of the same line and in *feel,* Lee (line 37), and *sea* (lines 40 and 41). Also, the long *i* sound of *rise* and *eyes* (lines 36), *night-tide* and *side* (line 38) and *bride* (line 39) is repeated in *bright* (line 36), *lie* (line 38), *my* and *life* (line 39), and *by* (lines 38, 40, and 41). The *o* in *moon* (line 34) is repeated in *tomb* (line 41) and is closely related to the sound in *beautiful* (lines 35 and 37).

   Repetition can be seen in "Annabel Lee" in the phrase "kingdom by the sea," which appears in lines 2, 8, 14, 20, and 24. The word "love" is repeated in lines 6, 9, 11, and 27.

6. *Rhyme* is evident in both poems, both end rhyme and internal rhyme. This can be seen in the last stanza of "Annabel Lee": *beams* in line 34 rhymes with *dreams*; *rise* in line 36 rhymes with *eyes*. *Night-tide* and *side* in line 38 rhyme with each other and with *bride* at the end of line 39.

TONE

Introduction

Tone is the writer's or speaker's attitude toward the poem's subject or audience. Tone brings emotional power to a poem and is a vital part of its meaning. In spoken language, tone is conveyed through the speaker's inflections, and it may vary in many ways. Possible tones, for example, include *ecstatic, incredulous, despairing, bleak,* and *resigned.* A correct interpretation of a poem's tone is vital to a correct interpretation of its meaning. It is more difficult to discern tone in writing than in speech since inflection cannot be determined in text. To understand tone in verse, we must analyze all the poetic elements that we have discussed previously: imagery, simile, metaphor, irony, understatement, rhythm, sentence structure, denotation, connotation, and so forth. Tone is a combination of all the elements.

As you read the following poem, try to determine its tone.

Crossing the Bar

Sunset and evening star,
    And one clear call for me!
And may there be no moaning of the bar,
    When I put out to sea,

5 But such a tide as moving seems asleep,
    Too full for sound and foam,
When that which drew from out the boundless deep
    Turns again home.

Twilight and evening bell,
10   And after that the dark!
And may there be no sadness of farewell,
    When I embark;

For though from out our bourne of Time and Place
    The flood may bear me far,
15 I hope to see my Pilot face to face
    When I have crossed the bar.

—Alfred, Lord Tennyson

Questions to Consider:

1. What are the two different figures that the poet uses to stand for death?
2. What is the exact moment of death in each instance?
3. What kind of death is the poet wishing for here? Why does he say that he wants no "sadness of farewell"?
4. What is the "boundless deep"?
5. What is the tone of this poem?

Answers:

1. Each figure begins a section of the poem. The first occurs in line 1, "Sunset and evening star," while the second is found in line 9, "Twilight and evening bell."
2. In the first instance, death occurs "When that which drew from out the boundless deep/Turns again home" (lines 7–8). In the second, death occurs when the speaker has "crossed the bar" (line 16).
3. The poet is wishing for a death that causes "no sadness of farewell," a death that is neither painful nor protracted. He does not want extended leave-takings, nor people gathered around the bedside of a dying man.
4. The "boundless deep" is that which awaits us after death.
5. The tone is one of calm resignation since the speaker is peaceful and relaxed as he faces death.

Try your hand at this next poem. Read it through carefully, focusing on the tone.

One Dignity Delays for All

One dignity delays for all,
One mitred afternoon.
None can avoid this purple,
None avoid this crown.

Coach it insures, and footmen.
Chamber and state and throng;
Bells, also, in the village,
As we ride grand along.

What dignified attendants,
What service as we pause!
How loyally at parting,
Their hundred hats they raise!

How pomp surpassing ermine
When simple you and I
Present our meek escutcheon
And claim the rank to die!

—*Emily Dickinson*

Questions to Consider:

1. What is the "dignity" that "delays for all"?
2. What is being discussed in the second and third stanzas?
3. Look up the following words if you are not sure of their meaning: *mitred, escutcheon.*
4. What is the tone of this poem? How does this poem differ in tone from Tennyson's "Crossing the Bar"?

Answers:

1. This "dignity" is death.
2. The second and third stanzas discuss the actual process of dying.
3. *Mitred* means "raised to a high rank." The poet is using it to describe a very special afternoon, the afternoon of her death. An *escutcheon* is a shield with a coat of arms.
4. The tone of this poem is decidedly more playful than that of "Crossing the Bar."

METER

Introduction

Sound in verse is created by two elements: the rhythm of the poem's lines and the sound of its words. We have already discussed *meter*, the rhythm of a poem determined by the number of stressed and unstressed syllables, and the common varieties of meter, such as *iambic pentameter*. *Scanning* a poem is determining its rhythm or meter.

Review of Meter

Read this brief review to refresh your understanding of meter:

Meter

Type	Number of Stresses	Examples
diameter	2 stresses per line	Díe soón
trimeter	3 stresses per line	Dóst thou knów who máde thee?
tetrameter	4 stresses per line	Tell áll the trúth but téll it slánt
pentameter	5 stresses per line	Leáve me, O Lóve, which reáches bút to dusť
hexameter	6 stresses per line	Whićh, like a wóunded snaké, draǵs its slow lenǵth alonǵ.

Discussion

As we have said before, seldom does the pattern of a poem remain perfectly regular, for to hold too closely to one meter can cause monotony. Poets seek to avoid such monotony by shifting stresses, so that a poem written in iambic meter may have some feet that are spondaic and others that are trochaic. More importantly, the poet varies meter by making the poem's meaning and the speaker's voice move with the rhythm. These few lines from Matthew Arnold's "Dover Beach" show this process at work:

> The sea is calm tonight.
> The tide is full, the moon lies fair
> Upon the straits—on the French coast the light
> Gleams and is gone; the cliffs of England stand,
> Glimmering and vast, out in the tranquil bay.

The first statement meshes beautifully with the meaning of the first line. But the next overlaps the second line, so that you cannot stop reading on "fair," but must continue with "Upon the straits" to make sense of the line. After a pause, the thought continues through that line and half the next, then pauses more briefly, finishes the line with a slight pause, and comes to an end with the fifth line. The first and fifth lines are called *end-stopped*, because a longer pause is called for at the end of these lines.

In the same manner, the second, third, and fourth lines force your voice to continue on. These are called *run-on* lines. But end-stopped and run-on lines may contain internal pauses; there is one such pause after the word "full" in the second line. These pauses are called *caesuras*, and their placement can vary the rhythm, stress specific words and ideas, and give poetry the sound of the speaking voice.

Meter in Blake's "The Lamb" and "The Tyger" and in Arnold's "Dover Beach"

Blake's "The Lamb" and the "The Tyger" (see pages 66 and 63-64) offer a marked contrast to Arnold's "Dover Beach." Because of the many end-stopped lines and the regularity of their rhythm, the two Blake poems sound almost like incantations, very different from the gentle, musing tone of Arnold's poem. But even in these two poems Blake varies the length of lines and includes some caesuras and run-on lines. Here are some examples:

> What the hammer? what the chain?
> In what furnace was thy brain?
> What the anvil? what dread grasp
> Dare its deadly terrors clasp?

Blake holds himself to seven-syllable lines in "The Tyger" and a patterned alternation between trimeter and tetrameter lines in "The Lamb," while Arnold varies the length of the lines in "Dover Beach," the lines getting longer as the speaker's argument continues. It is also clear that all the lines quoted from both the Blake and Arnold poems end with stressed syllables. The rising voice at the end of a line creates what is called *rising rhythm*. In contrast, lines that end in unstressed syllables create a *falling rhythm*. "O wild West Wind, thou breath of Autumn's being" is an example of falling rhythm.

Look at the following poem to determine both its meter and meaning:

Pied Beauty

Glory be to God for dappled things—
   For skies of couple-colour as a brinded cow;
     For rose-moles all in stipple upon trout that swim;
Fresh-firecoal chestnut-falls; finches' wings;
5   Landscape plotted and pieced—fold, fallow, and plough;
   And áll trádes, their gear and tackle and trim.

All things counter, original, spare, strange;
   Whatever is fickle, freckled (who know how?)
    With swift, slow; sweet, sour; adazzle, dim;
10 He fathers-forth whose beauty is past change:
                Praise him.

—*Gerard Manley Hopkins*

Questions to Consider:

1. How do the examples of "dappled things" in lines 2–4 differ from those in lines 5–6? How do the examples in the first stanza (lines 2–6) differ from those in the second stanza (lines 7–9)?
2. What has Hopkins done to his first definition of "dappled things"?
3. In what way are all the images and examples unified?
4. How important is the speaker's vision of "pied beauty" to the poem?
5. What is the rhythm here?

Answers:

1. Lines 2–4 present specific examples of dappled things: line 2, skies; line 3, trout; line 4, chestnuts, and birds' wings. Lines 5–6, in contrast, present general descriptions: line 5, landscape; line 6, trades.

2. Hopkins has gone from the specific to the general to include all of creation as he sees it.

3. The images and examples are connected by theme and language. In the first stanza, the theme is that all of the universe is God's glory and reflection. In the second stanza, we see an echo of language techniques: line 5—"fold, fallow, and plough;" line 9—"swift, slow, sweet," etc.

4. The speaker's vision is the most important thing in the world to him, for he was a priest who saw God's hand in all.

5. This is an example of Hopkins's sprung rhythm, explained on page 14. Recall that Hopkins placed strongly accented syllables against unaccented ones to produce greater tension and emphasis within each line.

Chapter 6

Unrhymed and Rhymed Verse

UNRHYMED VERSE

Unrhymed verse is rather easy to classify and can be divided into three main types as follows:

- *Accentual verse*   This originated in the eighth century and is the earliest known kind of verse. *Beowulf* is an example of early accentual verse. Gerard Manley Hopkins's "Pied Beauty" is an example of nineteenth-century accentual verse.
- *Blank verse*   This unrhymed iambic pentameter, a sixteenth-century development, was made famous by Shakespeare.
- *Free verse*   A nineteenth-century development, this type of unrhymed verse can be found in the works of such poets as Walt Whitman, E.E. Cummings, Ezra Pound, and Denise Levertov.

RHYMED VERSE

Rhymed verse cannot be divided into three simple categories. There are those forms of rhymed verse with a fixed length: the *limerick* with five lines, the *sonnet* with fourteen lines, and the *villanelle* with nineteen lines. There are other forms that do not have a fixed number of lines, although almost all are composed of stanzas. While each stanza usually has a fixed length, the number of stanzas may vary, so that a poem can be any length at all. There are a series of patterns, though, that we can isolate and discuss in depth.

Two-line forms

- *Couplet*   A couplet is a stanza of two rhyming lines. A couplet is found at the end of an English sonnet to make the point and conclude the discussion. Here is an example of a final couplet from a Shakespearean sonnet:

    > So long as men can breathe or eyes can see,
    > So long lives this, and this gives life to thee.

Three-line forms

- *Triplet* or *tercet*   A triplet or tercet is composed of three rhyming lines, as this example shows:

    > He clasps the crag with crooked hands,
    > Close to the sun in lonely lands,
    > Ringed with the azure world, he stands.

- *Terza rima*   Terza rima is another three-line stanza form. Here, however, only the first and the last lines rhyme. When several stanzas of terza rima are grouped together, the middle line of one stanza will rhyme with the first and third lines of the following stanza. Here is an example:

    > O wild West Wind, thou breath of Autumn's being,
    > Thou, from whose unseen presence the leaves dead
    > Are driven, like ghosts from an enchanter fleeing,
    >
    > Yellow, and black, and pale, and hectic red,
    > Pestilence-stricken multitudes: O Thou,
    > Who chariotest to their dark wintry bed

Four-line forms

Quatrains   The quatrain is a stanza composed of four lines that may have several different rhyme schemes: the second and the fourth lines (*abcb*); the first and third, and the second and fourth (*abab*); the first and fourth and the second and third (*abba*); the first and second and the third and fourth (*aabb*). Any one of these patterns may be used, or they may be combined in any variation. Thus, you cannot assume that if the first few stanzas follow a certain pattern, the rest of the poem will continue that pattern. It is always best to check the rhyme in each and every line to make sure that the pattern follows what you have found. Here are some examples to study:

(*abcb*) When I was one-and-twenty
I heard a wise man say,
"Give crowns and pounds and guineas
But not your heart away;"

(*abab*) She even thinks that up in heaven
Her class lies late and snores,
While poor black cherubs rise at seven
To do celestial chores.

(*abba*) Earth hath not anything to show more fair!
Dull would be he of soul who could pass by
A sight so touching in its majesty
The city doth now, like a garment, wear.

(*aabb*) "O, Melia, my dear, this does everything crown!
Who could have supposed I should meet you in Town?
And whence such fair garments, such prosperi-ty?"—
"O didn't you know I'd been ruined?" said she.

THE NARRATIVE POEM

The narrative poem tells a story, recounting actions and events. As in a short story or a novel, the sequence of events in a narrative poem is called a *plot,* and it must be controlled and directed by the *narrator,* the person telling us the tale. The *point of view,* the position from which the narrative is recounted, must also be controlled; this is accomplished in part by the grammatical *person* in which the author chooses to write. Most stories and poems are told in the *first-person (I)* or the *third-person point of view (he/she/they).* In the first-person point of view, the narrator tells the story from the vantage point of a character in the story. In the third-person point of view, the narrator is recounting events from outside the plot. Narrative verse is less popular today, as more stories are told in prose (non-poetry) form.

The following is a famous example of a narrative poem. Read the poem and the analysis that follows:

My Last Duchess

That's my last Duchess painted on the wall,
Looking as if she were alive. I call
That piece a wonder, now: Frà Pandolf's hands
Worked busily a day, and there she stands.
5   Will 't please you sit and look at her? I said
"Frà Pandolf" by design, for never read
Strangers like you that pictured countenance,
The depth and passion of its earnest glance,
But to myself they turned (since none puts by
10   That curtain I have drawn for you, but I)
And seemed as they would ask me, if they durst,
How such a glance came there; so, not the first
Are you to turn and ask thus. Sir, 'twas not
Her husband's presence only, called that spot
15   Of joy into the Duchess' cheek: perhaps
Frà Pandolf chanced to say "Her mantle laps
Over my lady's wrist too much," or "Paint
Must never hope to reproduce the faint
Half-flush that dies along her throat": such stuff
20   Was courtesy, she thought, and cause enough
For calling up that spot of joy. She had
A heart—how shall I say?—too soon made glad,
Too easily impressed; she liked whate'er
She looked on, and her looks went everywhere,
25   Sir, 'twas all one! My favor at her breast,
The dropping of the daylight in the West,
The bough of cherries some officious fool
Broke in the orchard for her, the white mule
She rode with round the terrace—all and each
30   Would draw from her alike the approving speech,

Or blush, at least. She thanked men—good! But thanked
Somehow—I know not how—as if she ranked
My gift of a nine-hundred-years-old name
With anybody's gift. Who'd stoop to blame
35   This sort of trifling? Even had you skill
In speech—(which I have not)—to make your will
Quite clear to such an one, and say, "Just this
Or that in you disgusts me; here you miss,
Or there exceed the mark"—and if she let
40   Herself be lessoned so, nor plainly set
Her wits to yours, forsooth, and made excuse
—E'en then would be some stooping; and I choose
Never to stoop. Oh sir, she smiled, no doubt,
Whene'er I passed her; but who passed without
Much the same smile? This grew; I gave commands;
45   Then all smiles stopped together. There she stands
As if alive. Will 't please you rise? We'll meet
The company below, then. I repeat,
The Count your master's known munificence
Is ample warrant that no just pretense
50   Of mine for dowry will be disallowed;
Though his fair daughter's self, as I avowed
At starting, is my object. Nay, we'll go
Together down, sir. Notice Neptune, though,
Taming a sea horse, thought a rarity,
55   Which Claus of Innsbruck cast in bronze for me!

—Robert Browning

Discussion

This is a narrative poem, the Duke's story of his marriage and his wife's
death. Browning uses a technique called a *dramatic monologue,* which
enables readers to feel almost as though they were overhearing the Duke
speaking. From the Duke's conversation, we are able to piece together
the situation, both past and present, and we are able to see what sort of
person the Duke really is and what sort of person his wife was. By the
end of the poem, we are even able to see what the poet thought of them
both.

Line-by-line analysis

Lines 1–2   Addressing an unidentified audience, the Duke discusses a portrait of his "last Duchess." The word "last" hints that the Duke may have had more than one previous wife and also suggests that he is once again shopping for a new wife. We know immediately that she is dead from the phrase "Looking as if she were alive" in line 2.

Lines 3–4   The word "piece," used to refer to the painting, also suggests that the Duke considered his wife little more than a commodity, something to acquire as one would any other possession. The Duke is very impressed with the painting and makes sure to mention the painter—and more than once. This reveals that the Duke admires works of art and that he is very conscious of status. Already we can tell that he treasures objects above people.

Lines 5–10   The Duke is eager to talk about the look on his former wife's face. It is also important that he tells us that he is the only one allowed to uncover her portrait. Even in death, he is in control, the one to allow her to be seen.

Lines 11–24   In line 14, the Duke says that it was not only his presence that called "that spot /Of joy" to her cheek. She had what he calls "A heart…too soon made glad" (line 22), and she liked "whate'er/She looked on" (lines 23–24). This caused him great distress, for he is used to being the one in control, the one—and the only one—able to call forth her joy.

Lines 25–30   These lines reinforce the Duke's distress, as he tells us that his admiration was, to the Duchess, the same as the sunset or a gift of a bough of cherries. He feels that he should have been the only one to please her and resents all the other things that caused her joy. He also says that the Duchess was gracious and kind, easy to please, and in sharp contrast to the Duke, content with the simple pleasures of life.

Lines 31–43   Lines 31–34 tell us that the Duke bitterly resented the way the Duchess seemed to rank all gifts the same. What right had she to rank the gift of his name (in marriage) with anyone else's gift, he asserts. He was unwilling to speak to her about her graciousness to all and his feelings about it, for he believed that he could never stoop to correct her. His pride prevented him from voicing his feelings.

Lines 44–46   The Duchess, happy with life, smiles at each and all. The Duke, furious with what he perceives to be a slight, gives commands, "Then all smiles stopped together" (line 45). This line is brilliantly juxtaposed with the next, "There she stands/As if alive," so we know that his command destroyed her, directly or indirectly. Perhaps he deprived her of the daily pleasures that give life its savor—beauty of nature, human company—or perhaps he did something even more heinous.

Lines 47–53   Here we learn that the Duke has been addressing someone sent by the Count to arrange a marriage between the Count's daughter and the Duke. The Duke smoothly asserts that his main goal is the Count's "fair daughter," but he fully intends to obtain a fitting dowry in the deal.

Lines 54–56   As they walk down the stairs, the Duke points out another one of his possessions, a bronze statue of Neptune "Taming a sea horse." Neptune has tamed the sea horse much as the Duke tamed his "last Duchess," destroying her spirit through his unbending pride.

The Duke emerges as arrogant and ruthless, determined to have his will prevail regardless of the cost. That his childlike wife would find innocent pleasure in commonplace events is insufferable to such an egoist, and so he "gives commands" that reassert his will—and destroy his wife's.

LYRIC VERSE

As stated earlier, lyric verse was originally a term used to describe any short poem meant to be sung to the music of a lyre, but the term has come to mean any short poem, regardless of meter or rhyme scheme, that expresses an emotion or records a thought rather than tells a story. Probably the most common emotion in lyrics is love, or the despair brought about by unreturned love, though grief and pain are also frequent subjects. The following lyric is from a sixteenth-century songbook:

> Western wind, when wilt thou blow,
> The small rain down can rain?
> Christ, if my love were in my arms,
> And I in my bed again!

The lyric flourished in the sonnets and songs of the Renaissance, enjoyed a rebirth in the nineteenth century, and has remained the most common form of verse today. There are many different kinds of lyrics. Here is a summary of the most popular forms:

Lyric type	Description
complaint	a long expression of dissatisfaction, usually to a loved one
dirge	a short funeral lament
elegy	a melancholy or mournfully contemplative poem
epigram	a brief witty expression
monody	a longer and more complex funeral poem
ode	a short poem characterized by heroic or elevated emotions
pastoral	any poem dealing with country life, usually concerning a shepherd
satire	a longer diatribe against folly or stupidity
sonnet	a fourteen-line poem expressing emotion
threnody	a funeral poem

Here is a famous lyric poem by Elizabeth Barrett Browning.

Sonnet 43

How do I love thee? Let me count the ways.
I love thee to the depth and breadth and height
My soul can reach, when feeling out of sight
For the ends of Being and ideal Grace.
I love thee to the level of everyday's
Most quiet need, by sun and candlelight.
I love thee freely, as men strive for Right;
I love thee purely, as they turn from Praise.
I love thee with the passion put to use
In my old griefs, and with my childhood's faith.
I love thee with a love I seemed to lose
With my lost saints—I love thee with the breath,
Smiles, tears, of all my life!—and, if God choose,
I shall but love thee better after death.

—*Elizabeth Barrett Browning*

THE ODE

The *ode* has a regular rhythmic pattern, although its meter and verse lengths may vary from time to time. Originally a song in honor of gods, there are now three main types of odes:

- *Pindaric or regular odes* These odes have three parts: a *strophe* (where the chorus danced while singing), an *antistrophe* (where the chorus retraced the same pattern while singing), and the *epode* (where the chorus sang without dancing). Within these fixed divisions there are lines of uneven length. More modern Pindaric odes include Gray's "The Progress of Poesy" and Wordsworth's "Ode: Intimations of Immortality."

- *Horatian or homostrophic odes*   This type of ode has one repeated stanza, but the stanza may vary in its form. Examples include Marvell's "Horatian Ode Upon Cromwell's Return from Ireland," Collins's "Ode to Evening," and Keats's "Ode to Autumn."
- *Irregular odes*   These odes tend to disregard the strophe and stanza rules of the model, the Pindaric ode. They thus tend to show greater flexibility with regard to length, meter, and rhyme and so are the most popular form.

The ode that follows is by William Wordsworth, one of the leaders of the Romantic movement in England. This ode uses both rhyme and rhythm to great advantage and also manages to keep a freshness of style and tone that combine to make it pleasant reading even today, long after it was written. Trace the way the poet develops his arguments and notice how the poem has been shaped to echo his ideas. See how the different stanzas reflect the speaker's change in emotion.

Intimations of Immortality from Recollections of Early Childhood

> The Child is Father of the Man;
> And I could wish my days to be
> Bound each to each by natural piety.

1

There was a time when meadow, grove, and stream,
The earth, and every common sight,
        To me did seem
    Apparelled in celestial light,
5 The glory and the freshness of a dream.
It is not now as it hath been of yore;—
        Turn wheresoe'er I may,
            By night or day,
The things which I have seen I now can see no more.

2

10   The Rainbow comes and goes,
        And lovely is the Rose,
        The Moon doth with delight

Look round her when the heavens are bare,
    Waters on a starry night
15   Are beautiful and fair;
   The sunshine is a glorious birth;
   But yet I know, where'er I go,
That there hath past away a glory from the earth.

3

Now, while the birds thus sing a joyous song,
20   And while the young lambs bound
      As to the tabor's sound,
To me alone there came a thought of grief:
A timely utterance gave that thought relief,
    And I again am strong:
25 The cataracts blow their trumpets from the steep;
No more shall grief of mine the season wrong;
I hear the Echoes through the mountains throng,
The Winds come to me from the fields of sleep,
    And all the earth is gay;
30   Land and sea
   Give themselves to jollity,
    And with the heart of May
    Doth every Beast keep holiday;—
      Thou Child of Joy,
35 Shout round me, let me hear thy shouts, thou happy
  Shepherd-boy!

4

Ye blessed Creatures, I have heard the call
    Ye to each other make; I see
The heavens laugh with you in your jubilee;
    My heart is at your festival,
40   My head hath its coronal,
The fulness of your bliss, I feel—I feel it all.
      Oh evil day! if I were sullen
      While Earth herself is adorning,
        This sweet May-morning,
45   And the Children are culling

On every side,
In a thousand valleys far and wide,
Fresh flowers; while the sun shines warm,
And the Babe leaps up on his Mother's arm:—
50   I hear, I hear, with joy I hear!
—But there's a Tree, of many, one,
A single Field which I have looked upon,
Both of them speak of something that is gone:
The Pansy at my feet
55   Doth the same tale repeat:
Whither is fled the visionary gleam?
Where is it now, the glory and the dream?

5

Our birth is but a sleep and a forgetting:
The Soul that rises with us, our life's Star,
60   Hath had elsewhere its setting,
And cometh from afar:
Not in entire forgetfulness,
And not in utter nakedness,
But trailing clouds of glory do we come
65   From God, who is our home:
Heaven lies about us in our infancy!
Shades of the prison-house begin to close
Upon the growing Boy,
But He beholds the light, and whence it flows,
70   He sees it in his joy;
The Youth, who daily farther from the east
Must travel, still is Nature's Priest,
And by the vision splendid
Is on his way attended;
75 At length the Man perceives it die away,
And fade into the light of common day.

6

Earth fills her lap with pleasures of her own;
Yearnings she hath in her own natural kind,
And, even with something of a Mother's mind,

80   And no unworthy aim,
        The homely Nurse doth all she ca
    To make her foster-child, her Inmate Man,
        Forget the glories he hath known,
    And that imperial palace whence he came.

7

85 Behold the Child among his new-born blisses,
    A six years' Darling of a pigmy size!
    See, where 'mid work of his own hand he lies,
    Fretted by sallies of his mother's kisses,
    With light upon him from his father's eyes!
90 See, at his feet, some little plan or chart,
    Some fragment from his dream of human life,
    Shaped by himself with newly-learnèd art;
        A wedding or a festival,
        A mourning or a funeral;
95   And this hath now his heart,
        And unto this he frames his song:
            Then will he fit his tongue
    To dialogues of business, love, or strife;
        But it will not be long
100   Ere this be thrown aside,
        And with new joy and pride
    The little Actor cons another part;
    Filling from time to time his "humorous stage"
    With all the Persons, down to palsied Age,
105 That Life brings with her in her equipage;
            As if his whole vocation
            Were endless imitation.

8

    Thou, whose exterior semblance doth belie
        Thy Soul's immensity;
110 Thou best Philosopher, who yet dost keep
    Thy heritage, thou Eye among the blind,
    That, deaf and silent, read'st the eternal deep,
    Haunted for ever by the eternal mind,—

Mighty Prophet! Seer blest!
115   On whom those truths do rest,
Which we are toiling all our lives to find,
In darkness lost, the darkness of the grave;
Thou, over whom thy Immortality
Broods like the Day, a Master o'er a Slave,
120   A Presence which is not to be put by;
Thou little Child, yet glorious in the might
Of heaven-born freedom on thy being's height,
Why with such earnest pains dost thou provoke
The years to bring the inevitable yoke,
125   Thus blindly with thy blessedness at strife?
Full soon thy Soul shall have her earthly freight,
And custom lie upon thee with a weight,
Heavy as frost, and deep almost as life!

9

O joy! that in our embers
130   Is something that doth live,
That nature yet remembers
What was so fugitive!
The thought of our past years in me doth breed
Perpetual benediction: not indeed
135   For that which is most worthy to be blest;
Delight and liberty, the simple creed
Of Childhood, whether busy or at rest,
With new-fledged hope still fluttering in his breast:—
Not for these I raise
140   The song of thanks and praise;
But for those obstinate questionings
Of sense and outward things,
Fallings from us, vanishings;
Blank misgivings of a Creature
145   Moving about in worlds not realised,
High instincts before which our mortal Nature
Did tremble like a guilty Thing surprised:
But for those first affections,
Those shadowy recollections,

150   Which, be they what they may,
    Are yet the fountain light of all our day,
    Are yet a master light of all our seeing;
        Uphold us, cherish, and have power to make
    Our noisy years seem moments in the being
155 Of the eternal Silence: truths that wake.
        To perish never;
    Which neither listlessness, nor mad endeavor,
        Nor Man nor Boy,
    Nor all that is at enmity with joy,
160 Can utterly abolish or destroy!
        Hence in a season of calm weather
        Though inland far we be,
    Our Souls have sight of that immortal sea
        Which brought us hither,
165   Can in a moment travel thither,
    And see the Children sport upon the shore,
    And hear the mighty waters rolling evermore.

10

    Then sing, ye Birds, sing, sing a joyous song!
        And let the young Lambs bound
170   As to the tabor's sound!
    We in thought will join your throng,
        Ye that pipe and ye that play,
        Ye that through your hearts to-day
        Feel the gladness of the May!
175 What though the radiance which was once so bright
    Be now for ever taken from my sight,
        Though nothing can bring back the hour
    Of splendour in the grass, of glory in the flower;
        We will grieve not, rather find
180   Strength in what remains behind;
        In the primal sympathy
        Which having been must ever be;
        In the soothing thoughts that spring
        Out of human suffering;
185   In the faith that looks through death,
    In years that bring the philosophic mind.

11

And O, ye Fountains, Meadows, Hills, and Groves,
Forebode not any severing of our loves!
Yet in my heart of hearts I feel your might;
190   I only have relinquished one delight
To live beneath your more habitual sway.
I love the Brooks which down their channels fret,
Even more than when I tripped lightly as they;
The innocent brightness of a new-born Day
195   Is lovely yet;
The Clouds that gather round the setting sun
Do take a sober colouring from an eye
That hath kept watch o'er man's mortality;
Another race hath been, and other palms are won.
200   Thanks to the human heart by which we live,
Thanks to its tenderness, its joys, and fears,
To me the meanest flower that blows can give
Thoughts that do often lie too deep for tears.

—William Wordsworth

Discussion

In form, this poem is an irregular ode, for the stanzas vary among themselves, following the argument of the poem. The meter is iambic, although the length of the lines and the rhythm shift. The poem discusses the relationship among the human soul, nature, and immortality. It suggests that we know what immortality is after death, but even more interesting, it says that we could also know immortality before birth: "But trailing clouds of glory do we come/From God, who is our home" (lines 64–65). It revels in the joy that a child sees in the world of nature as well as laments the fact that the child turns his attention to earthly things, quickly dulling that initial joy. But even so, the conclusion is not sorrowful, as the poet passes beyond mourning this loss to celebrating the joys that the mature human soul is capable of appreciating.

THE SONNET

The most popular of the defined poetic forms is the sonnet. It is a lyric poem of fourteen lines, written in iambic pentameter (five accents per line). There are two main sonnet forms.

- *The Petrarchan sonnet*   The first type of sonnet was originated by the Italian poets in the thirteenth century and reached its final form a century later in the works of Petrarch; thus, it came to be called the Petrarchan or Italian sonnet. The first eight lines, called the octave, rhyme *abbaabba* and present the subject of the poem; the final six lines, called the sestet, rhyme *cdecde* and resolve the problem or situation set forth in the first eight lines.
- *The Shakespearean sonnet*   The English poets of the sixteenth century altered the rhyme scheme of the Italian sonnet, creating an *abab/ cdcd/ efef/ gg* pattern, which has come to be called the Shakespearean or English sonnet. Some claim that the Shakespearean sonnet is easier to write, for no sound needs to be written more than twice. On the other hand, it has been suggested that the Italian sonnet has a smoother flow and is more graceful.

Originally, both forms of the sonnet came into the language as love verse, but sonnets have been used for many different themes and subjects. A close look at the models that follow will show this variety. Examine each sonnet and decide (1) if it is a Petrarchan or Shakespearean sonnet; (2) the rhyme scheme; (3) the poet's theme or main idea; (4) how the figurative language and poetic devices enhance the theme.

Sonnet 116

Let me not to the marriage of true minds
Admit impediments; love is not love
Which alters when it alteration finds,
Or bends with the remover to remove:
O, no, it is an ever-fixèd mark,
    That looks on tempests and is never shaken;
    It is the star to every wand'ring bark,

Whose worth's unknown, although his highth be taken.
Love's not Time's fool, though rosy lips and cheeks
Within his bending sickle's compass come;
Love alters not with his brief hours and weeks,
But bears it out even to the edge of doom.
    If this be error, and upon me proved,
    I never writ, nor no man ever loved.

—William Shakespeare

Sonnet 73

That time of year thou mayst in me behold
When yellow leaves, or none, or few, do hang
Upon those boughs which shake against the cold,
Bare ruined choirs, where late the sweet birds sang.

In me thou see'st the twilight of such day
As after sunset fadeth in the west;
Which by and by black night doth take away,
Death's second self that seals up all in rest.
In me thou seest the glowing of such fire,
That on the ashes of his youth doth lie,
As the deathbed whereon it must expire,
Consumed with that which it was nourished by.
    This thou perceiv'st, which makes thy love more strong,
    To love that well, which thou must leave ere long.

—William Shakespeare

Longfellow's Sonnets

Henry Wadsworth Longfellow wrote a series of sonnets with especially deep feeling. In July of 1861, his wife was tragically burned to death despite Longfellow's frantic attempts to save her. Overcome with grief, he sought relief in his work and set forth an especially difficult task for himself—to translate into English Dante's *Divine Comedy.* The poem has three parts that describe Dante's fictional journey into Hell,

Purgatory, and Paradise. In his version, Longfellow opened each section with two sonnets. While Longfellow claimed that his purpose here was to describe Dante's verse as a cathedral, he is seemingly using Dante's poem to comfort himself in his grief. The two sonnets that follow preface part of Longfellow's translation.

Oft have I seen at some cathedral door
   A laborer, pausing in the dust and heat,
   Lay down his burden, and with reverent feet
   Enter, and cross himself, and on the floor
Kneel to repeat his paternoster o'er;
   Far off the noises of the world retreat;
   The loud vociferations of the street
   Become an undistinguishable roar.
So, as I enter here from day to day,
   And leave my burden at his minister gate,
   Kneeling in prayer, and not ashamed to pray,
The tumult of the time disconsolate
   To inarticulate murmurs die away,
   While the eternal ages watch and wait.

* * * * *

How strange the sculptures that adorn these towers!
   This crowd of statues, in whose folded sleeves
   Birds build their nests; while canopied with leaves
   Parvis and portal bloom like trellised bowers,
And the vast minster seems a cross of flowers!
   But fiends and dragons on the gargoyled eaves
   Watch the dead Christ between the living thieves,
   And, underneath, the traitor Judas lowers!
Ah! from what agonies of heart and brain,
   What exultations trampling on despair,
   What tenderness, what tears, what hate of wrong,
What passionate outcry of a soul in pain,
   Uprose this poem of the earth and air,
   This medieval miracle of song!

Read the following poems and answer the questions that follow. As you read, focus on the elements you have just learned:

Sonnet 10

Death, be not proud, though some have call'd thee
Mighty and dreadful, for thou art not so;
For those whom thou think'st thou dost overthrow
Die not, poor Death, nor yet canst thou kill me.
From rest and sleep, which but thy pictures be,
Much pleasure; then from thee much more must flow,
And soonest our best men with thee do go,
Rest of their bones, and soul's delivery.
Thou art slave to fate, chance, kings, and desperate men,
And dost with poison, war, and sickness dwell,
And poppy or charms can make us sleep as well
And better than thy stroke; why swell'st thou then?
One short sleep past, we wake eternally,
And death shall be no more; Death, thou shalt die.

—John Donne

Questions to Consider:

1. Who is the speaker addressing?
2. According to the speaker, what different things affect the subject of the poem?
3. What is the speaker's attitude toward the subject of the poem?
4. How does this affect the meaning of the poem?
5. What is the form of this poem? How is the form suited to the content? Specifically, how do the last two lines of the poem explain the theme and the author's attitude?
6. What do you think moved the poet to write this poem?

Answers:

1. The speaker is addressing death, which is personified as a living thing.
2. The speaker charges that Death's supposed power is undercut (and finally destroyed) by the following realities: (1) We derive much pleasure from rest and sleep, which mirror Death; (2) Death is at the mercy of "fate, chance, kings, and desperate men"; (3) Death lives with "poison, war, and sickness"; (4) Drugs ("poppy") and magic

spells ("charms") induce sleep as well as Death; (5) Death is but a brief passage into eternal existence.

3. The speaker's attitude is bold and defiant as he attacks Death's supposed invulnerability.

4. The speaker's attitude reinforces the poem's meaning: that Death is not to be feared, for Death is but a brief passage to an eternal life.

5. The poem is a sonnet, as the title indicates. The final two lines indicate the sonnet's "turn," summing up the speaker's main idea.

6. While answers will vary, it seems likely that the poet has lost a loved one or fears his own death.

Read the following sonnet. Then explain what the poet wished to be loved for and why she feels this way.

Sonnet 14

If thou must love me, let it be for nought
Except for love's sake only. Do not say,
"I love her for her smile—her look—her way
Of speaking gently,—for a trick of thought
That falls in well with mine, and certes brought
A sense of pleasant ease on such a day"—
For these things in themselves, Beloved, may
Be changed, or change for thee,—and love, so wrought,
May be unwrought so. Neither love me for
Thine own dear pity's wiping my cheeks dry,—
A creature might forget to weep, who bore
Thy comfort long, and lose thy love thereby!
But love me for love's sake, that evermore
Thou may'st love on, through love's eternity.

—*Elizabeth Barrett Browning*

Answer:
The first two lines state that the author wishes to be loved for "nought [nothing]/Except for love's sake only." This is picked up again in the final two lines, "But love me for love's sake, that evermore/Thou may'st love on, through love's eternity." She wishes to be loved for "love's sake"

because if love is not based on mere physical attraction ("her smile," "her look," "her way/Of speaking gently"), then it will be able to endure for eternity.

Show how the two parts of the following sonnet, "How Soon Hath Time," are united by the theme. You will have to:

- find and explain the two parts of the poem
- describe the theme
- show how time unites the poem

How Soon Hath Time

How soon hath Time, the subtle thief of youth,
    Stol'n on his wing my three and twentieth year!
    My hasting days fly on with full career,
    But my late spring no bud or blossom shew'th.
5 Perhaps my semblance might deceive the truth
    That I to manhood am arrived so near,
    And inward ripeness doth much less appear,
    That some more timely-happy spirits endu'th.
    Yet be it less or more, or soon or slow,
10   It shall be still in strictest measure even
    To that same lot, however mean or high,
Toward which Time leads me, and the will of Heaven;
    All is, if I have grace to use it so,
    As ever in my great Taskmaster's eye.

—*John Milton*

Answer:

The first part of the poem, lines 1–6, discuss the outward changes the speaker has undergone. Such changes are reflected in the statement, "Perhaps my semblance might deceive the truth/That I to manhood am arrived so near" (lines 5–6), which shows, in the word "semblance," the *outward* changes time has caused. The second part of the poem concerns *inward* changes, as found in the phrase "inward ripeness" (line 7). The theme, stated in the final four lines, is that the changes the speaker has experienced are the will of Heaven.

What appalls Captain Ahab in Herman Melville's epic novel *Moby Dick* is the whiteness of the whale Moby Dick. Twentieth-century poet Robert Frost works with that symbolism in the following poem. Discuss the symbolism of Frost's "Design" and explain how the "whiteness" relates to the poem's theme. Then show how the form of "Design" is suited to the poem's theme.

Design

I found a dimpled spider, fat and white,
On a white heal-all, holding up a moth
Like a white piece of rigid satin cloth—
Assorted characters of death and blight
5 Mixed ready to begin with morning right,
Like the ingredients of a witches' broth—
A snow-drop spider, a flower like a froth,
And dead wings carried like a paper kite.

What had that flower to do with being white,
10 The wayside blue and innocent heal-all?
What brought the kindred spider to that height,
Then steered the white moth thither in the night?
What but design of darkness to appall?—
If design govern in a thing so small.

—*Robert Frost*

Answer:
Trace the white items listed in the first four lines: spider, fat, and white; white heal-all; moth, looking like a white piece of cloth. All these items are linked by the comment in line 4: "Assorted characters of death and blight." These images of death and decay continue: "witches' broth," "dead wings." These images are pulled together in the final two lines of the poem as the speaker expresses surprise that there is some power governing the formation and design of items even as small and seemingly insignificant as the ones he lists. If there is a hand behind even these petty items, what then rules our lives which we hold so very significant?

The poem is a sonnet, having fourteen lines with the following rhyme scheme:

white	*a*
moth	*b*
cloth	*b*
blight	*a*
right	*a*
broth	*b*
froth	*b*
kite	*a*
white	*a*
heal-all	*c*
height	*a*
might	*a*
appall	*c*
small	*c*

This is a variation on the Italian (Petrarchan) sonnet, whose rhyme scheme is *abbaabba cdecde.* This pattern is followed through the octave (the first eight lines) but breaks form in the sestet to *acaacc,* with a final rhyming couplet, the *cc.* A strong case could be made that the poet follows the pattern in the first eight lines to use the form to reinforce the meaning: the poem's rigid *form* echoes life's fixed *design.* In the conclusion, however, the poet breaks with the sonnet's rhyme scheme to create a new pattern. This is reflected in the theme of design ruling even the smallest item in nature—but *not* Frost's creation, the poem.

Read the poem below and answer the questions that follow. Explain the meaning of "fire" and "ice." Why does the poet conclude that "ice" will also suffice for destruction?

Fire and Ice

Some say the world will end in fire,
Some say in ice.
From what I've tasted of desire
I hold with those who favor fire.

But if it had to perish twice,
I think I know enough of hate
To say that for destruction ice
Is also great
And would suffice.

—Robert Frost

Answer:
Fire represents passion and desire, that which heats up our lives. Ice is cold, hard hate, devoid of the heat of passion. The poet concludes that hate is strong enough to cause the destruction of the world, even though most people might conclude that desire, passionate fire, is most apt to set things aflame.

Chapter 7

Sample Essays for Analysis

Below is a selection of sample poems and essays for your analysis. Read the poems through several times, noting such elements as symbols, figurative language, meter, rhyme, and theme. Then write your own essays. After you have completed your work, read through the sample essays and compare them to your own.

Sample Question 1

Read the two poems that follow. Then compare the tone of the first poem to the tone of the second one. Show their similarities and differences. Use specific lines from each poem to support your points. *Time: 45 minutes.*

A Man Adrift on a Slim Spar

A man adrift on a slim spar
A horizon smaller than the rim of a bottle
Tented waves rearing lashy dark points
The near whine of froth in circles.
5   God is cold.

The incessant raise and swing of the sea
And growl after growl of crest
The sinkings, green, seething, endless
The upheaval half-completed.
10   God is cold.

The seas are in the hollow of The Hand;
Oceans may be turned to a spray
Raining down through the stars
Because of a gesture of pity toward a babe.
15 Oceans may become gray ashes,
Die with a long moan and a roar
Amid the tumult of the fishes
And the cries of the ships.
Because The Hand beckons the mice.

20 A horizon smaller than a doomed assassin's cap,
Inky, surging tumults
A reeling, drunken sky and no sky
A pale hand sliding from a polished spar.
                              God is cold.

25 A puff of a coat imprisoning air:
A face kissing the water-death
A weary slow sway of a lost hand
And the sea, the moving sea, the sea.
                              God is cold.

                                        —Stephen Crane

When I Consider How My Light Is Spent

When I consider how my light is spent,
    Ere half my days, in this dark world and wide,
    And that one talent which is death to hide
    Lodged with me useless, though my soul more bent
5 To serve therewith my Maker, and present
    My true account, lest he returning chide;
    "Doth God exact day-labor, light denied?"
    I fondly ask; but Patience to prevent
That murmur, soon replies, "God doth not need
10   Either man's work or his own gifts; who best
    Bear his mild yoke, they serve him best. His state
Is kingly. Thousands at his bidding speed

And post o'er land and ocean without rest:
They also serve who only stand and wait."

—*John Milton*

Sample Essay

The tone of the first poem, "A Man Adrift on a Slim Spar," differs markedly from the tone of the second poem, "On His Blindness." While each poet describes an omnipotent God, in the first poem the Supreme Being is cold and indifferent; in the second poem, He is warm and compassionate.

On a literal level, the first poem describes a man vainly clinging to a slender scrap of wood in the middle of the raging ocean. The poet carefully stacks the odds against the drowning man: the spar is "slim" (line 1), the "horizon smaller than the rim of a bottle" (line 3). God is all-powerful, the poet says, able to control the seas in the hollow of His hand, to make of them what He wishes. The ocean may be transformed into a gentle "spray/Raining down through the stars" because God feels compassion toward a child, or it may become a merciless storm that brings fishes and sailors alike to their brutal ruin—all at God's whim. The man adrift in the ocean is doomed, his "pale hand sliding from a polished spar" as his face kisses "the water-death" and he sinks from sight. God is not actively against this man—or any man, for that matter—the poet says; rather, He is merely "cold," indifferent to man's suffering and torment in the bitter cold ocean of life. The tone reflects this view of God and so "A Man Adrift on a Slim Spar" has a bitter and harsh tone. The second poem, however, has a very different tone.

"On His Blindness" offers a much more traditional view of God and His relationship to humanity, echoed in its more traditional form. A sonnet written with an *abba/abba/cde/cde* rhyme scheme, the poem depicts God as every bit as powerful as in the first example but as a great deal more compassionate. The speaker begins by lamenting the loss of his vision, which renders his one talent, the ability to write, virtually useless. He is distraught because he desires above all else to be able to serve God through his writing, to be able to represent himself fully, and to glorify God through his prose and verse. God will not force him to perform tasks beyond his ability, he knows, such as compose verse without sight, but nevertheless he wishes to contribute to God's glorification. This is in marked contrast to the first poet's attitude, for he has no desire to serve God in any capacity. God has allowed the speaker in Crane's poem only a slim spar and then He has turned His back. The first speaker, then, never even discusses the notion of dedicating himself to God. In Milton's sonnet, on the other hand, God, in the form of Patience, reassures the speaker that those who "stand and wait" also serve His will. God is king, the second poem implies, and thousands vie for the chance to serve His bidding. The speaker in this poem need not worry that he has failed to properly honor his God.

The two situations are very different, as are the attitudes of the speakers. In the first poem, the speaker sees God as cold and indifferent and thus the tone is bitter and harsh. In the second poem, in contrast, the speaker sees God as compassionate and understanding; thus, the tone is gentle and reassuring.

Analysis of Essay

The introduction gets right to the point and answers the question fully. The writer also makes sure to mention each poem by name so there will not be any confusion about the subject of the essay. Further, the writer specifically indicates the tone for each poem.

The plot summary provided in the second paragraph clearly contributes to answering the question, for it focuses on the theme. There is good sentence variety, especially in the varied use of punctuation. The writer shows a continued awareness of stylistic elements by carefully selecting a number of vivid adjectives, such as "vainly," "slender," and "fierce." These help make the essay clear and precise. In addition, there are many specific examples drawn from the text of the poems, and each is used to make the point. From the line "God is not actively against this man…" to the end of the paragraph, the point is clearly stated and is well supported by good specific examples.

The third paragraph, on Milton's sonnet, also addresses the question. The two paragraphs are tied together by the last line of the second paragraph, lending unity to the whole essay. The specific examples clearly state the tone, and the last portion of the paragraph makes a clear comparison between the two poems.

The conclusion sums up all that has been stated before and makes the point clearly. In sum, this is a logical, stylistically competent essay. The writer shows a clear understanding of the poems and a sure grasp of writing techniques.

Sample Question 2

Read the following poem and discuss the author's theme. Be sure to answer these questions in your analysis:

- What is the tone of the first twelve lines of the poem?
- What is the tone of the final two lines?
- How are they different?
- How is the form of the sonnet suited to this method of development?

Time: 30 minutes.

Sonnet 130

My mistress' eyes are nothing like the sun;
Coral is far more red than her lips' red;
If snow be white, why then her breasts are dun;
If hairs be wires, black wires grow on her head.
5   I have seen roses damasked, red and white,
But no such roses see I in her cheeks;
And in some perfumes there is more delight
Than in the breath that from my mistress reeks.
I love to hear her speak, yet well I know
10   That music hath a far more pleasing sound;

I grant I never saw a goddess go;
My mistress, when she walks, treads on the ground.
And yet, by heaven, I think my love as rare
As any she belied with false compare.

—*William Shakespeare*

Sample Essay

The tone of the first twelve lines of Shakespeare's Sonnet 130 contrasts sharply to the tone of the final two lines, and this difference establishes the tone of the entire poem. The first twelve lines of the poem parody the form and content of the typical love verse, as the woman fails to measure up to any of the traditional emblems of love and devotion. Thus, her eyes, the time-honored windows to the soul, lack the clear radiance of the sun, and her lips, the deep, rosy tint of coral. Her skin is mottled and dark; her hair, coarse wires. The tone is playful and mocking, as Shakespeare inverts all the accepted tools of the love sonneteer's trade to construct a series of false analogies. The tone of the final two lines, however, differs sharply.

This is an Elizabethan or English sonnet, and often the final two lines (called the "couplet") serve to sum up the meaning of the preceding twelve lines and establish the author's tone. Such is the case here, for the couplet's tone and meaning differ markedly from the rest of the poem. These two lines are serious, not playful and light, as the author declares his love for the lady he has just pilloried at the stake of false comparisons. He wrote this poem, he says here, to parody her tendency to compare their love to objects and in so doing, to establish false analogies. Their love is a rare and a serious thing, he states, not to be diminished through "false compare."

The sonnet form is well suited to the difference in tone, as the couplet at the end allows the author the opportunity to sum up the first twelve lines and establish the theme. Here, he abjures the parody of the first twelve lines to firmly and seriously declare his love.

Analysis of Essay

This essay answers the question fully, with style and grace. The first line weaves together both aspects of the question—tone and theme—and alludes to the question of sonnet form as well. The next sentence follows logically, and the ones after that provide clear examples of the speaker's point. Next, the writer moves to the final two lines and displays a clear knowledge of the conventions of the Elizabethan sonnet. The writer then shows, through specific examples, how the final two lines differ in tone from the first twelve, concluding by showing how the sonnet form is well suited to the theme of the poem.

Sample Question 3

Read the following two poems and discuss each of the following:

- How do the two authors view old age? How do their views differ from each other?
- What effect does this different view have on the tone of each poem?
- What differences in style can you see in each poem?

Time: 25 minutes.

The Last Leaf

I saw him once before,
As he passed by the door,
   And again,
The pavement stones resound
5 As he totters o'er the ground
   With his cane.

They say that in his prime,
Ere the pruning-knife of Time
   Cut him down,
10 Not a better man was found
By the Crier on his round
   Through the town.

But now he walks the streets,
And he looks at all he meets
15   So forlorn
And he shakes his feeble head
That it seems as if he said,
    "They are gone."

The mossy marbles rest
20 On the lips that he has pressed
    In their bloom,
And the names he loved to hear
Have been carved for many a year
    On the tomb.

25 My grandmamma has said—
Poor lady—she is dead
    Long ago;
That he had a Roman nose,
And his cheek was like a rose
30   In the snow.

But now his nose is thin,
And it rests upon his chin
    Like a staff,
And a crook is in his back,
35 And a melancholy crack
    In his laugh.

I know it is a sin
For me to sit and grin
    At him here;
40 But the old three-cornered hat,
And the breeches—and all that,
    Are so queer!

And if I should live to be
The last leaf upon the tree
45   In the spring,
Let them smile, as I do now
At the old forsaken bough
      Where I cling.

—Oliver Wendell Holmes

Terminus

It is time to be old,
To take in sail:—
The god of bounds,
Who sets to seas a shore,
5 Came to me in his fatal rounds,
And said: 'No more!
No farther shoot
Thy broad ambitious branches, and thy root.
Fancy departs: no more invent;
10 Contract thy firmament
To compass of a tent.
There's not enough for this and that,
Make thy option which of two;
Economize the failing river,
15 Not the less revere the Giver,
Leave the many and hold the few.
Timely wise accept the terms,
Soften the fall with wary foot;
A little while
20 Still plan and smile,
And,—fault of novel germs,—
Mature the unfallen fruit.
Curse, if thou wilt, thy sires,
Bad husbands of their fires,
25 Who, when they gave thee breath,

Failed to bequeath
The needful sinew stark as once,
The Baresark marrow of thy bones,
But left a legacy of ebbing veins,
30   Inconstant heat and nerveless reins,—
Amid the Muses, left thee deaf and dumb,
Amid the gladiators, halt and numb.'

As the bird trims to her gale,
I trim myself to the storm of time,
35   I man the rudder, reef the sail,
Obey the voice at eve obeyed at prime:
'Lowly faithful, banish fear,
Right onward drive unharmed;
The port, well worth the cruise, is near,
40   And every wave is charmed.'

—*Ralph Waldo Emerson*

Sample Essay

"Terminus" is a calm, dignified, realistic statement of an old man accepting his advanced age and his fast-approaching death. The first line—"It is time to be old"—can be cited to support this. Lines 39–40—"The port, well worth the cruise, is near,/And every wave is charmed"—also illustrate the speaker's dignified attitude toward old age and death. It is a poem of serious and deep contemplation. "The Last Leaf," in sharp contrast, is initially light and playful in tone. Most of the figures of speech in "The Last Leaf" are comic, with the exception of those used in the last verse. Images such as "the pruning-knife of Time" has "cut him down" (lines 8–9) and "his nose…rests upon his chin/Like a staff" (lines 31–33) are examples of the initial comic tone of this poem. But the character in the last stanza is lonely, for the last leaf upon the tree in the spring is even more poignant than the last leaf in autumn. This leaf, a symbol for the old man, has been able to survive the ravages of the winter. Now, surrounded by new life bursting forth, it can only wither away and die. Note that in the last stanza the speaker abandons his distance from the character and now identifies with him, looking ahead to the time when he, too, will be "the last leaf upon the tree/In the spring."

Chapter 8

For Additional Reading

Below you will find a list of recommended poets and the poems for which they are especially well known. In some instances specific works will be listed; in other cases, just the poet's name will be included, meaning any of their poems are recommended. This list makes no claims for inclusiveness; instead, its aim is to provide you with a way to continue your exploration and enjoyment of poetry.

EIGHTH CENTURY

anonymous	*Beowulf*

THIRTEENTH/FOURTEENTH CENTURIES

anonymous	ballads
Chaucer	poems
Francesco Petrarca (Petrarch)	sonnets

SIXTEENTH CENTURY

Christopher Marlowe	*Doctor Faustus*
William Shakespeare	sonnets
Sir Philip Sidney	sonnets
Edmund Spenser	sonnets
François Villon	"Ballade"

SEVENTEENTH CENTURY

Anne Bradstreet	poems
John Donne	poems
John Dryden	poems
John Gay	poems

George Herbert	poems
Robert Herrick	poems
Samuel Johnson	poems
Richard Lovelace	poems
Andrew Marvell	poems
John Milton	*Paradise Lost*
Alexander Pope	"Ode to Solitude," poems
Edward Taylor	"Huswifery," "Upon a Wasp Chilled with Cold," poems

EIGHTEENTH CENTURY

Charles Baudelaire	*Flowers of Evil*
William Blake	"Songs of Innocence," "Songs of Experience"
Robert Burns	poems
Thomas Gray	"Elegy Written in a Country Churchyard"
Phillis Wheatley	"To His Excellency, George Washington," poems

NINETEENTH CENTURY

Matthew Arnold	"Dover Beach"
Elizabeth Barrett Browning	*Sonnets from the Portuguese*, poems
Robert Browning	poems
William Cullen Bryant	"To a Waterfowl," "Thanatopsis," poems
Lord Byron	"She Walks in Beauty," poems
Lewis Carroll	"Jabberwocky"
Samuel Taylor Coleridge	"Kubla Khan"
Emily Dickinson	poems
Ralph Waldo Emerson	poems
Edward Fitzgerald	"The Rubaiyat of Omar Khayyam of Naishapur"
Thomas Hardy	poems

Gerard Manley Hopkins	poems
A. E. Housman	"To an Athlete Dying Young," "Loveliest of Trees," "When I Was One-and-Twenty"
Victor Hugo	"June Nights," poems
John Keats	"Ode on a Grecian Urn," "Ode to a Nightingale"
Rudyard Kipling	"Recessional," poems
Henry Wadsworth Longfellow	poems
Herman Melville	poems
George Meredith	"Lucifer in Starlight," poems
Edgar Allan Poe	poems
Christina Rossetti	"A Birthday," poems
Dante Gabriel Rossetti	"Silent Noon," poems
Percy Bysshe Shelley	"Ode to the West Wind," poems
Alfred, Lord Tennyson	"Ulysses," poems
Henry David Thoreau	poems
Walt Whitman	*Leaves of Grass*
William Wordsworth	poems

TWENTIETH CENTURY

Anna Akhmatova	poems
Yehuda Amichai	"The Diameter of the Bomb," poems
W.H. Auden	"Musée des Beaux Arts," "In Memory of W.B. Yeats," poems
Imamu Amiri Baraka	"An Agony. As Now."
John Berryman	"Homage to Mistress Bradstreet," "Dream Songs"
Elizabeth Bishop	poems
Louise Bogan	poems

Joseph Brodsky	poems [Nobel Prize]
Gwendolyn Brooks	"The Beat Eaters," "We Real Cool," poems
Hart Crane	poems
Stephen Crane	"Black Riders and Other Lines," "War Is Kind"
Countee Cullen	poems
E.E. Cummings	poems
Ruben Dario	"Sonatina"
James Dickey	"Falling," poems
Hilda Doolittle (HD)	poems
Rita Dove	poems
Robert Duncan	poems
T. S. Eliot	"The Waste Land," "The Hollow Men," "The Love Song of J. Alfred Prufrock," "The Journey of the Magi," *Four Quartets,* poems [Nobel Prize]
Robert Frost	"Stopping by Woods on a Snowy Evening," "The Road Not Taken," poems
Allen Ginsberg	"Howl," "A Supermarket in California"
Robert Graves	"One Hard Look," "She Tells Her Love While Half Asleep," poems
Thom Gunn	poems
Robert Hayden	poems
Seamus Heaney	"Follower," "Shore Woman," poems
Geoffrey Hill	poems
Langston Hughes	poems
Ted Hughes	"Pike," "Hawk Roosting," "The Horses," poems

Randall Jarrell	"The Death of the Ball Turret Gunner"
Galway Kinnell	poems
Philip Larkin	poems
D. H. Lawrence	poems
Denise Levertov	poems
Philip Levine	poems
Frederico García Lorca	"The Guitar," "Rider's Song"
Audre Lorde	poems
Robert Lowell	poems
Archibald MacLeish	"You, Andrew Marvell"
Louis MacNeice	"The Sunlight in the Garden," "Sunday Morning," poems
Edgar Lee Masters	*Spoon River Anthology*
W. S. Merwin	poems
Edna St. Vincent Millay	poems
Czeslaw Milosz	"Encounter," poems [Nobel Prize]
Gabriel Mistral	"Rocking," poems [Nobel Prize]
Marianne Moore	poems
Pablo Neruda	"Ode to My Socks," "Horses" [Nobel Prize]
Lorine Niedecker	poems
Charles Olson	poems
Simon J. Ortiz	"Sand Creek," poems
Octavio Paz	"Fable," "Concord"
Sylvia Plath	"Daddy," "Lady Lazarus," "Ariel"
Ezra Pound	*The Cantos,* poems
John Crowe Ransom	poems
Adrienne Rich	poems
E. A. Robinson	"Richard Cory," "Minniver Cheevy," "Mr. Flood's Party"

Theodore Roethke	poems
Alberto Rios	"Advice to a First Cousin"
Nelly Sachs	"The Swan," poems [Nobel Prize]
Carl Sandburg	poems
George Serferis	"I Am Sorry," poems [Nobel Prize]
Anne Sexton	poems
Stevie Smith	"Not Waving But Drowning," "Pretty," poems
Cathy Song	poems
Wole Soyinka	poems
Wallace Stevens	"The Snow Man," poems
Dylan Thomas	"Do Not Go Gentle Into That Good Night," "Fern Hill," "The Force That Through the Green Fuse Drives the Flower," poems
Jean Toomer	poems
Derek Walcott	"Sea Grapes," "Sunday Lemons"
Robert Penn Warren	poems
Richard Wilbur	poems
William Carlos Williams	"The Dance," "The Red Wheelbarrow," "The Yachts," poems
Elinor Wylie	poems
William Butler Yeats	"Leda and the Swan," "When You Are Old," "The Second Coming," poems [Nobel Prize]
Yevgeny Yevtushenko	poems